MONEY *for* LIFE

*How You Can Create
a Financial Plan for
Life & Align Your
Investments with
Your Values*

Stephen R. Bolt

with W. TERRY WHALIN

VFN Publishing
Nashville, Tennessee

Money for Life

By Stephen R. Bolt

Copyright © 2000 by Stephen R. Bolt
Revised 2001

ISBN 0-9677356-1-0

04 03 02 01 00   10 9 8 7 6 5 4 3 2 1

Published by Values Financial Network, Inc.
210 Jamestown Park Drive, Suite 100
Brentwood, TN 37027

Cover design by Steve Diggs & Friends, Nashville, TN
Cover Photo: Jerry Atnip
Text design and composition by Whisner Design Group, Tulsa, OK

DEDICATION

This book is dedicated to
Forrest Stephen William Bolt.
Through his short life and untimely death,
I was given a glimpse of Christ that
pierced my soul and gave me life.
I am eternally grateful to my son.

Money for Life

Walk into any bookstore or surf the net and you'll discover books, guides, newsletters, and sites crammed with information about money.

If there's so much information out there, what are we still looking for? We're looking for what these books, guides, newsletters, and sites fail to instill in their general financial advice–recognition of our personal values in our financial and investment planning.

"When you pause to consider and then grasp that your life is literally a gift from God, you become better equipped to live a life of purpose and meaning instead of settling for a default existence," reveals financial expert, Stephen Bolt. "We waste tremendous energy in our attempts to gain greater efficiency—and end up racing toward the wrong goal."

Money for Life was written because of the conspicuous absence of teaching about values-based financial planning. The peace, power, and financial freedom that everyone is struggling to find is actually available to you right now— regardless of your current financial situation. But first you must step out of the noise and begin building your financial plan as an individualized reflection of who you are.

Discover how to...

- Apply all of life's resources toward living the abundant life God has given you.
- Sort through your options and transform your dreams into goals.
- Develop a financial plan that wholeheartedly supports your goals.
- Create a meaningful investment program that reflects your personal values.

More than just helping you attain greater confidence in managing your money, paying less taxes, and accumulating more assets, *Money for Life* will help you uncover your true motivation for life. If you miss this fundamental step of the financial planning process in your rush to win the game of having more money, in the final analysis, it won't really matter how much money you accumulate, because you will have ultimately lost—and lost big!

The great truth is that you can have it all. The key is in approaching your finances in the right order, and recognizing that the first step, the one that most people miss, is the most important.

Then, when all of the steps are in order, you won't believe how fast you'll get to where you always wanted to go!

STEPHEN R. BOLT was off and running in the financial services industry in 1981. As a three-time NCAA All-American, Stephen's drive for excellence and his award-winning performance have not been limited to athletics. In 1985, he became the top representative nationally with a $35 billion Lutheran financial services company, and then achieved the top position twice more in 1995 and 1998 with two independent broker dealers.

Stephen earned his Certified Financial Planner designation from the CFP Board of Standards in 1994 and served as a consultant for a $155 million retirement plan in 1997. In 1998, Stephen formed Shepherd Advisory Services, an SEC Registered Investment Advisor, and launched the Shepherd Values Family of Mutual Funds. At the same time, he created the Values Financial Network, a trade association of financial advisors who adopted values-based investing to their financial planning practice. In late 2000, the VFN was sold to Regan Holding Corp, which also hired Stephen as executive director for the VFN. Additionally, Stephen was appointed by RHC as chief marketing officer for his new initiative, MoneyAndValues.com, one of the first Internet-based platforms that allowed investors to evaluate the values represented by their mutual funds and seek more appropriate alternatives.

Today, Stephen is president and CEO of Shepherd Financial Services, and president of Harpeth Financial Group, a wholesaler of values-based products using the MoneyAndValues.com platform. He is a leading consultant to investment firms and insurance companies in the rapidly developing values-based investing niche, and has been featured on hundreds of radio programs, CNNfn, Bloomberg TV, as well as periodicals including *Global Investment Technology* and *Mutual Fund Market News*. He is the author of two books, *Money for Life* (1999), and *Your Money, Your Values* (2000).

He and his wife, Elizabeth, along with their three children, Ruby, Ann-Rachel and Reagan, in Brentwood, Tennessee.

Stephen can be contacted at <sbolt@moneyandvalues.com>.

• • • • • •

W. TERRY WHALIN is a freelance writer who lives in Colorado Springs, Colorado.

Table of Contents

FOREWORD

Stephen Bolt is a Christian individual who strives to live his life on purpose. One element among many in Stephen's life purpose is to enable and encourage others to define God's purpose for their own lives instead of blindly accepting a prescription for purpose suggested by someone else.

But encouraging an individual to define God's purpose for his life is not what makes Stephen's book unique. Rather, *Money for Life* is unique because of its practical guidelines for translating *purpose* to *action*. Stephen shows the committed individual how to take appropriate steps to make sure his investments are in line with his values.

While we realize we can never fully achieve God's intentions for our lives, those of us who believe in His grace also choose to respond to His gift of grace by making a renewed effort. This book provides several tools to help us in that process.

As Richard Houston, president of the Christian Community Foundation, observed, "Stephen Bolt is among the new breed of financial professionals who 'put their money where their heart is.' *Money for Life* is about more than money. It will give us all a fresh, new perspective about living life on purpose in pursuit of the really important things."

Thank you, Stephen.

— Bruce Piltingsrud
Vice President,
Market Development
Lutheran Brotherhood

ACKNOWLEDGEMENTS

Because it would be nearly impossible to list all the people who gave of themselves to help this book become reality, I offer a resounding thank-you to all my clients, employees, family, and friends.

I do want to make special mention of a few people who played key roles, however. I thank my parents, Tom and Nori Bolt, who instilled in me the importance of values. Professionally I owe much to my good friend Bruce Piltingsrud, always my intellectual superior, who not only allowed me his audience—to which I could dialogue about my values-based investing ideas—but who also tenaciously nurtured the development of these ideas from concept to form. I also thank Nina May for helping me see the need for such a book and Terry Whalin for patiently counseling me through the process.

Finally, I thank my wife, Libby, who helped me carve out enough space and time to think, do research, and write *Money for Life,* who supported me through my frustrations, and who has partnered with me in our journey of purposeful life.

Is Your Financial Foundation
Built on Sand or Rock?

My new business venture was progressing dramatically. It would bring a fresh perspective to the financial services industry, complete with a new series of values-based products. Yet as exciting as this was, it was no more exciting than what was happening in my personal life.

Our family isn't that different from other American families in the late twentieth century. We're a blended family. My wife, Elizabeth Ann "Libby" Monette, had an eighteen-month-old daughter, Ruby, from a previous marriage. I had a daughter from a previous marriage too, a twenty-two-year-old daughter whom my former wife and I had adopted when she was age ten. Now, just several months after our marriage, Libby and I were expecting our first child. The prospect brought me unbounded happiness and excitement. In our plans, this new child would blend our two families into one.

A year earlier, one of my clients who was preparing to experience the birth of his first child had decided to attend each of his wife's visits to the doctor during her pregnancy. It helped him to celebrate their pregnancy on an intimate level. I liked the idea, and so even before Libby got pregnant I determined that the doctor visits would be high priority for me.

As the months went by, I interrupted my business schedule and changed my travel plans so I could accompany Libby on her visits to the ob-gyn. I'll never forget the first time I saw my son on the video monitor during an ultrasound examination. The baby's rapid heartbeat alarmed me. As a former competitive runner, I knew quite a bit about heart rate, blood pressure, and cardiovascular activity. The baby's heartbeat ranged between 140 and 150 beats a minute. This would be taxing for a normal adult, so I expressed my concern.

"It's completely normal and expected," the nurse reassured us. At return visits for sonograms we continued to peer into Libby's womb to see how our child was developing. On one visit I noticed that his head had grown, and I could see his spine. Another time I noticed the pronounced ribs, the curled fingers, and the little legs that were crossed. We became acquainted with our new son and named him Forrest Stephen William Bolt.

Even at night, Libby and I celebrated Forrest. We would snuggle close together, and Forrest would interrupt our sleep through his kick to her stomach and, consequently, my back. Or sometimes Forrest got the hiccups and I could feel his movements all the way over on my side of the bed. We cheered every little action of this new life.

Ruby was also looking forward to her new baby brother. After Libby's baby shower, Ruby sorted through various toys and selected ones she thought he would appreciate. In preparation for his arrival from the hospital, she piled the toys in various places around our home. One toy in particular captured her attention—a little rattle that Ruby held out to give Forrest at the hospital.

As her pregnancy neared the end, Libby made preparations. She had readied clothes for every season of our baby's first year, and she had even put a bed beside the crib in case she needed to stay in his room while nursing him. Together we picked out a rocker for the room and attached little mobiles over the crib. Libby hand-painted block letters over the doors to both Ruby's and Forrest's bedroom.

My expectations for our new family life were huge. One particular time the excitement really hit me. I was on a flight to Portland, Oregon, in our ninth month of pregnancy when the anticipation of our new family filled me. I found myself searching for some paper to write down my feelings so that I could share them with Libby. Although my business initiatives were consuming virtually all the energy I could muster and were finally showing signs of real growth, they couldn't match my elation for our new child.

On August 11, 1998, I was returning to my home in Nashville, Tennessee, from my last meeting of the week, three time zones away. Hectic days had been complemented by sleepless nights as I wrestled with the tough challenges of a young company. And early in the day, the planes on the West Coast had been delayed by weather, which caused a domino effect on the airlines. I flew from one airport to the next trying to get back to Nashville. My lovely wife was a welcome sight at the gate when I was finally able to walk off the last plane and into the terminal.

I absorbed Libby's warm smile, and we headed to baggage pickup and out to the car. Not only was this a pleasant end to a stressful week, but it would be the last travel for me for a while. I had crammed all the "absolutely essential" travel into these last days in order to clear my schedule for Forrest's birth and his first few weeks in his new family.

On the drive home, we chitchatted about a number of things and got caught up on our lives. Once home, we plopped down on some furniture in the kitchen. While I grabbed a snack, Libby recounted the activities of the household over the last few days. I loved returning home, and I relished the brief respite from the demands of the business world.

Libby and I had developed a habit of talking about Forrest as if he were already a part of our family. We knew what he looked like from the sonograms, and we even knew something about his personality. When I was in town and Libby and I talked on the phone during the day, I always asked how he was doing or what he was up to at that moment. She would say, "Oh, he's doing great today, kicking up a storm" or "He had the hiccups this morning." Sometimes when he was active she'd say, "It feels like he's practicing somersaults!"

Now as the clock read almost midnight and we were still engaged in our conversation, I casually asked how Forrest was doing. Instead of her usual response, she paused and gave me a puzzled look. "Well, I'm not quite sure. I've not felt him for most of the day."

Immediately I felt some growing concern from her response. We reconstructed her activities of the day with the goal of discovering when she last felt movement. After talking about it, she couldn't recall a specific time. Neither one of us wanted to consider the ramifications of the lack of movement. So we talked about other things and eventually headed to bed.

Before turning out the lights, however, we returned to our concern about Forrest and his lack of movement. Libby maintained an extensive inventory of books on childbirth and pregnancy, which she consulted. Finally I said, "Libby, maybe you should call the doctor."

On the phone, the doctor on call suggested an immediate trip to the hospital in order to monitor the baby. After long hours of meetings and travel and no sleep, a trip to the hospital at one in the morning was the last thing I would have chosen to do. But not knowing whether the baby was in good health, neither of us could have slept.

We dressed, walked out into the dark night, got into our white Ford Expedition, and headed toward the hospital. The streets were practically deserted. We made the trip in silence, each being caught up in our own thoughts and prayers. Each of us had a nagging fear that we didn't want to validate with spoken words.

We parked in the emergency area and walked through the automatic doors into the hospital. Libby and I went to the third floor, where the nursery, the neonatal unit, and the delivery rooms were located. The hallways were pink and decorated with photos of babies born during the last month. The doctor had called ahead to prepare for our arrival, and the nurses were expecting Libby.

A nurse settled Libby into a recovery room that had several beds separated by curtains. She took Libby's vital signs and asked a series of questions. Next the nurse brought out a heart-monitoring device and positioned the belt around Libby's waist. No activity registered as the nurse moved the belt around Libby's abdomen. The nurse then looked up and asked, "Have you had any difficulty finding a heartbeat in the past?"

"No," Libby responded. Her answer gave voice for the first time to our fear about Forrest. After several minutes of attempting to find the heartbeat, the nurse summoned the resident doctor on duty and called for ultrasound equipment to be wheeled in. The doctor moved the sensor back and forth across Libby's abdomen, but we didn't see any movement on the screen. Throughout the procedures, Libby and I maintained eye contact to show the depth of our concern, but we didn't talk.

I'd been with Libby a number of times in the past for these procedures, so I knew what we were supposed to see.

But this time was different. There he was, so still, so silent. In the past, Forrest had always moved around, turned over, stretched, or crossed his legs. But not now. He was quiet. He was so still. I didn't want to believe my eyes. I couldn't.

Time and space became suspended as two thoughts came searing into my mind: *Oh, my God, my son is dead* and *Oh, my God, poor Libby.*

After six or seven minutes, the doctor finally turned the equipment off, looked over at us, and said, "I'm sorry. I can't find a heartbeat. I'm so sorry." In a split second, I felt the indescribable emotions of rage, pain, and unfulfilled hopes. All our plans, the baby showers, the birth announcements, the baby's new furniture, our new family...all gone. Dashed. Over. Just like that.

My immediate concern was for Libby. She was in disbelief, shock, fear, and pain. Tears streamed down her face. I wanted nothing more than to comfort her, but like so many bad dreams where you want to move and find that you simply can't, I didn't have anything to give. After a minute or two, I finally leaned over and whispered, "You will see him again, and you will know him when you meet him." As a Christian, I knew these to be facts, but in this context they were totally unrehearsed. I attribute them to God's spirit moving within me.

In a few hours, I knew the doctors would perform a C-section on Libby, and at that point I would have been awake continuously for over thirty hours. When the doctor asked if we wanted to see our son after the surgery, we both said no.

We were in such emotional distress, caught in a quagmire of emotions that we found ourselves totally without the ability to make any decision. This was uncharted ground for us, so unexpected. We just wanted to get through this awful situation and get home. The medical personnel allowed me to be with Libby during the procedure.

While in the operating room holding Libby's hand, I suddenly had a strong desire to see Forrest. Libby was under the effects of anesthesia and was in and out of consciousness. How could I go ahead and hold my son but respect her wishes too? How would I explain it to her? As the doctors performed the C-section, I saw the tears in their eyes at this unspeakable injustice. Then they whisked Forrest out of the room. I had to say something to the doctors, but first I had to say it to Libby. Fortunately she was awake, so I leaned over to her and said, "Hon, I've changed my mind. I want to see him." Again, I attribute grace to what happened next. To my surprise, she looked up at me and said, "I do too."

The professionals at Baptist Hospital are familiar with this process of parents first wanting nothing to do with the baby and then changing their minds. They kept Forrest nearby and waited until we were ready to see him. While Libby was in recovery, they brought him to us. He was beautiful. He was a full nineteen and a half inches long and had brown curly hair. He was perfect in every way except one: He didn't breathe. The grievance counselor helped us. She put together a beautiful case with pictures of Forrest, locks of his hair, and something akin to a birth certificate.

One by one various relatives came to the room, each wanting the chance to meet baby Forrest. When my parents came, I could not be with them. The emotional pain was too great. I pointed down the hall instead and watched as they went in to meet him. We also had to wrestle with whether Ruby should see her brother. She had been so excited, so prepared for his birth. After much prayer and counsel, we finally decided to allow it. Libby's mother brought Ruby to the hospital to meet her baby brother. She came into the room wearing a big smile and holding a rattle that she had picked out for her little brother. Ruby sat in my lap and asked if she could hold baby Forrest. The nurse placed Forrest, all bundled up in a baby blanket, into Ruby's arms. Immediately she looked up at me and, breaking the tense moment said, "Dad, he looks just like you." Ruby was so excited. She now knew her baby brother. There was no sense of remorse for her. The decision for her to see Forrest has been a good one, and one for which we—and Ruby—will be thankful for the rest of our lives.

My emotions were raw. I hadn't slept in nearly two days, and I had barely eaten. I was past the point of exhaustion, so I excused myself and walked outside the hospital to get some fresh air. My head was spinning.

Forrest's death was the most painful experience of my life. I felt as if a horse had kicked me in the stomach. At the same time, as I responded to people who offered their condolences, I found that a well inside me had begun bubbling up with a feeling that almost wasn't real. What was it? Was it…joy? Yes, it was. Strange as it may seem, I found that the enormous pain I was experiencing had a balancing counterpart—joy. Although the emotional and physical pain had not receded, my spirit, ironically, had begun to soar. I could not explain it. It was as if God's Spirit had divinely touched me. But how? Where? Why?

I traced my feelings to the wellspring. I felt God's presence and found a deep spiritual insight that I had never before experienced. In an instant, I felt incomprehensible gratitude to Him for His love. And in that same instant, I knew that Forrest was with God, which was the specific result of the plan of redemption, promised to us all by the God of the universe. This was no fantasy! It was as if I saw His whole plan, from start to finish, in one continuous moment. I saw the betrayal of His children in the Garden of Eden when Satan convinced Adam and Eve to turn away from their Father.

And I saw that as a result of their pride, their desire to "be like God," Satan began destroying God's creation with all forms of sin: disease, poverty, greed, hate, and, ultimately, death. Our holy and perfect Creator could have left us to fend for ourselves, to suffer the eternal consequences of sin. But He didn't. He designed a plan to save us, to give us, once again, life with Him. God's plan of redemption required a sacrifice, but not from us.

The sacrifice had to be blameless, perfect. It could only be His Son, Jesus Christ.

Jesus' humiliating torture and death on the cross removed forever all blemish of sin from those who believed. When Jesus, being both God and man, became our substitute sacrifice, He thwarted Satan's attack and numbered his days. Death no longer meant the end. Jesus was not only the sacrifice, but He was also the firstborn of the resurrection, so that all who believe in Him might be united with Almighty God, Father and Creator, through the Holy Spirit now, and then in life eternal. My God, what depth of love!

As I thought about the death of Forrest, I realized that the entire salvation story was manifested in this beautiful, little child. Forrest was an innocent little boy conceived within a world of sin. The injustice of his death is the effect of sin. The perfect world that God created for us is long gone, replaced by one plagued with the consequences of sin. But through the Cross, God has guaranteed humankind's reunion with Him. And now I also have the guarantee that my son lives in that perfect world in the arms of his heavenly Father.

I was overjoyed by the incredible clarity of my understanding of God, given to me through the Holy Spirit. Never before had I felt such a combination of confidence, joy, and peace, at least not as the world knows those terms. My confidence was not in me; rather it was in Him.

The joy I experienced was different from feelings of happiness. Who, after all, could be happy while suffering through the death of their child? The joy I found was in the knowledge that God's incredible love didn't desert us when His creation failed Him. Instead He overcame our failure by sacrificing His own Son so that you and I—and Forrest— could join Him in that perfect world planned for us.

And the peace I felt didn't spring from an absence of stressful circumstances. Hardly. The peace was deeper, more satisfying, eternal. That peace helped me to understand for the first time what Jesus meant when He repeatedly used the phrase *kingdom of God*. Truly the Holy Spirit had given me entrance to this kingdom.

As Libby and I moved on with our life, we experienced God's grace in so many ways. Our church and community supported us continuously. Many times people who had shared a similar experience and had written to us moved us to tears. "Dear Stephen and Libby, You don't know us, but we would like you to know we share your grief…" We experienced a generous outpouring of love and support that was testimony to the mystery of God's love working through His people.

The experience of losing Forrest changed our lives. Beyond the pain of experiencing the death of a child, I have learned the truth about life. Please understand that the truth I speak is God's and not mine. God revealed it to us through His words in the Bible and His ever-present Spirit.

I have been a believer all my life, but I only now appreciate the difference between knowing something on an intellectual level and experiencing it on a spiritual level. Although I had previously taught numerous Bible studies and had held virtually every position there is to hold in a church, I had never before experienced God in this manner. As Job said so long ago, "My ears had heard of you, but now my eyes have seen you" (Job 42:5). I had only known God *intellectually,* which is good enough for salvation. But I came to realize that my intellectual knowledge didn't help me in my temporal life. Experiencing God is transforming. God's Word was revealed to us not merely to "inform," but rather to be the means to "transform."

I now understand why the apostle Peter could be seen shouting on the street corners of Jerusalem about God's love and plan of redemption following his experience at pentecost. I now understand why the apostle Paul could not hold himself back from proclaiming the Good News of salvation even at the threat of execution. I know why he could be found singing hymns of praise while chained, starved, and beaten. I now understand how intellectual understanding can become a faith that transforms life itself. Now all the Scriptures that proclaim "a new life in Christ," "the kingdom of God," and "being transformed" make complete sense to me.

My life will never again be the same.

I related the personal story of Forrest's short life in the hope that it will help awaken in you a better understanding as it did in me. The God of the Bible is real. So is sin. Both sin and God are forces to be reckoned with, not only for the life to come but also for the present life. There is—literally—supernatural power in this recognition. And through this power, you can face challenges, move mountains, and reach goals. As you tap into this power resource, you will begin to see things differently and live a life of purpose. This resource is available to you right now and without cost—it's free. You no longer need to feel that you are alone. You are not. The God of the universe has given His peace, His forgiveness, and His Spirit to you. Our heavenly Father knew you before your birth and has made provision for you. God has provided you with life, resources, and relationships—and His ever-present Spirit.

Despite the lies, perversions, and depth of Satan's influence that we see all around us, God is still present. As the apostle Paul told the church at Rome nearly two thousand years ago, God takes any disaster, any tragedy, any injustice and makes good come from it (paraphrase of Romans 8:28). Trust God. And trust His promises—they are real, and they are for you. Plan with Him, in His will, and your life will enter a new phase of confidence, joy, and peace.

Now that you know that God will never let you down, that His Spirit is always with you, and that there is nothing you could ever do to take away His forgiveness, how do you feel? The battle is over; the war is already won. God Himself gave you life. Your birth was not a chance event. You are here to bear His image to the world. And what does that image look like? It looks peaceful, confident, and assured of love. It is purposeful. And it is creative. Are you surprised by this last attribute? Look around you. The colors, the landscapes, the vegetation, and the personalities all reflect God's creativity. And that leads me to the most critical question of this book.

How will you bear God's image of love, purpose, and creativity in your life? However you go about living your life in answer to that question, one thing is certain: Because economics is part of our physical world, money will be required. You will need to find answers to such questions as...

- How much money will I need?
- When will I need it?
- In what amounts will I need it?
- For how long?
- How do I reflect my values in the way I invest?

Since struggle and pain have been inherent in life since Eden, it's a pretty safe assumption that you've been through some difficult times in your life. No one gets through life solely on easy terms.

My personal story about Forrest marks this book as distinct from others in the financial field. While many books are filled with the how-to's of financial planning, they altogether miss the most critical point, which involves purpose. *Money for Life* certainly includes specific advice for prudent financial planning, but the initial focus of this book is decidedly different. The idea of purpose is inherent in the term *financial planning*. Planning for what? Life? Yes, but be sure, absolutely sure, that you first understand precisely what your life is all about before you map out a strategy for getting there.

As you read the following chapters, you will find that my perspective is unmistakably Christian. At the core of my advice about financial management is my belief in Jesus Christ as the Son of God and Savior of the world. Please don't stop reading if you don't know Jesus. The information and financial management principles presented in this book will still be useful to you. Based on my two decades of work sharing professionally in the lives of hundreds of people, however, I am convinced that without tapping into God's will, you will not find the peace and the satisfaction in life that you are seeking. This is true regardless of how successful you are at financial management or anything else in your life.

CHAPTER 1

The Necessity
of a Life Plan

For almost two decades in the financial planning industry, I have explored the turf of financial advice. I have found that although many advisors offer sound financial advice, they omit an important element. All the data, charts, graphs, analyses, and strategies missed asking one simple question: "What is the motivation, reason, or purpose behind the need for financial planning?"

The motivation for financial planning goes beyond selecting the right mutual fund or following a financial plan that allows you to meet your objectives for funding your children's college education or to retire a few years earlier. Although we may choose to ignore our own mortality, ultimately each of us will some day face death. If we manipulate our finances to gain a few more days of enjoyment, will it really matter? No, it won't.

The only way our life will have purpose and meaning is in Christ. As we seek God's purpose for our life, our will becomes joined to His. Because we have purpose in Christ, we therefore resolve to manage sufficient resources for our physical life. I am convinced that only after you understand your driving purpose for life will you be in any kind of position to begin to undertake appropriate financial planning, using all the strategies, tactics, and tools available. Most of this book will deal with those tools and how they can be applied to your individual circumstances. But I have no personal interest in teaching the effective use of those financial tools without the overriding context of *living life on purpose.*

Jesus made clear this principle when He asked, "What good is it for a man to gain the whole world, yet forfeit his soul?" (Mark 8:36). As we choose a life in Christ and then live it in faith, we can, regardless of circumstances, act with purpose, confidence, and peace regarding our financial resources.

LIVING ON PURPOSE OR SIMPLY EXISTING?

Are you living on purpose or simply existing? Several years ago, Pastor David Callies, now the district president for the Mid-South District of the Lutheran Church Missouri Synod, told a story that illustrates this principle:

One cool fall evening, Grandfather sat near the fireplace with his thirteen-year-old grandson. As they stared into the fire, watching the flames lick the logs, Grandfather began a significant conversation with the innocent opening, "Jim, how's everything going?"

Jim looked up at Grandfather and said, "It's going well. I'm excited about some of my projects in science class, plus I'm having a good year on the football team. In fact, I'm on the first string, and the coaches are talking about putting me on the varsity team next year."

Grandfather smiled and recognized Jim's commitment to athletics and academics. "High school football is great. Are you planning on going to college?"

"Certainly," Jim responded. "I can't tell if I will get an athletic scholarship or not, but I'm looking into several colleges. One in particular has an excellent science program."

Dreaming about his grandson's life, Grandfather continued. "So in college, you will study science—kind of like your dad. Have you thought about going into a research field?"

"Yes," Jim agreed. "With a solid school background, I imagine I'll be able to get a corporate job."

Pushing it a bit further, Grandfather said, "Thought about a family?"

"I imagine that I will get married, but I'd wait until a couple of years after college. I've even dreamed about having a couple of children," Jim said. The pair talked and moved through several children, their education, and even Jim's plans to save money toward retirement.

After dreaming about the key elements in Jim's life, Grandfather asked a final key question of Jim, "So, you'll retire with plenty of money to do those things you want. Jim, then what?"

Pausing in deep thought, Jim finally said, "Well, I suppose then I'll die."

This sermon hit me as a financial planner. After all, what was I doing to help people live life in such a way that it was more than just financial resources? In the final analysis, wasn't I endorsing the idea that life was really about obtaining material riches and gaining a bit more of what America offered? Regardless of our career, health, or financial success, unless our life has purpose, it is nothing more than existence until death puts an end to it.

A few years ago, I watched a television presentation about Marlon Brando. The interviewer retraced for sixty minutes the highs, lows, excitement, pomp, and circumstances of this legendary figure. Finally, at the end of the interview, the reporter asked him, "So, if you were about to take your last breath, looking back over your life in all its fullness, what would you say?"

Marlon Brando thought a minute and then responded. "Whew! What was *that* all about?"

If it were not true, it would be funny.

Forrest's death was like a knock on the head with a theological two-by-four. I now know that there is meaning and purpose only in a life lived in Christ. Because Jesus Christ walked the earth, took my sins (and your sins) on the cross of Calvary, and rose from the dead, I have the power to live life on purpose. As we face the challenges of everyday life, remembering the magnitude of what God has done for us through His redemptive grace is a constant struggle. Phone calls, meetings, birthdays, bills, barking dogs, and everything else that makes up our daily life pull at us. Only through prayer, devotion, and the mutual support of other believers can we sustain the peace, confidence, and joy that transcend whatever life's circumstances throw at us.

I've read or heard a number of the life-planning speakers and authors who suggest that we find fulfillment and peace only to the extent that we are good stewards of our God-given time, talents, and treasures. But this formula-like approach still misses the mark. Let me give an example of the emptiness of this misguided resource management.

As a competitive runner early in my young adult life, I learned to combine my athletic abilities with my drive and self-determination. My first race was unforgettable. My nerves were so jangled that I couldn't stand still. In November 1969 I ran the Turkey Trot in Orlando, Florida.

Several months earlier, my father had given up smoking and taken up running. From time to time he would suggest that I run with him. For a few afternoons, we both ran but rarely together. I took off and ran a mile or two as fast as I could and then returned home to plunge into some other activity.

One night I watched Dad fill out the paperwork for his first race. I wondered how I would do in a race. I decided to see, so I entered in the junior high division. To my complete surprise and satisfaction, I not only won my first race, but I did so by thirty-two seconds!

I became the fastest miler in the nation, and various colleges across the United States offered full athletic scholarships. I decided to accept a scholarship from one of the Southeastern Conference schools, having a degree of loyalty for that region south of the Mason-Dixon line. After visiting the major schools of the SEC, I selected the University of Alabama. No one in the Southeastern Conference had yet broken the four-minute mile, and that became my all-consuming goal throughout college. Every other activity, including schoolwork, relation-ships, and fun, took second place to that goal. My goal was daunting and would not be achieved without total commitment. I knew my weight had to be perfect, so I continuously watched my diet and controlled my weight. My workouts were critical, so I constantly consulted my coaches and researched the records of great milers.

Every day when I got up and prepared for the morning run, I visualized breaking the four-minute mile. Throughout my day of classes, I daydreamed about that goal. My desire to break the four-minute mile consumed my thoughts during my afternoon workout and at night while listening to music before finally falling asleep. My goal spilled over to my teammates, and they were supportive. When a race day came, for example, my teammates positioned themselves at strategic points around the track. Keeping their eyes on the clock, they used hand signals to let me know if I was too far ahead or too far behind my intended pace. On several occasions, I came close to breaking the elusive four-minute barrier—running 4:03, 4:02, 4:01, and then 4:00 flat. Then one day, on the final leg of a distance medley relay race, I did it. I broke the four-minute mile! But because it was a relay race, it wasn't recorded in the record books. Nonetheless, the experience showed me that I was capable and ready to achieve my goal.

The next event on the schedule was the Southeastern Conference Championship at Louisiana State University in Baton Rouge. That indoor facility was my favorite in the conference. I was pumped and excited. Then, the day before the team was scheduled to travel to Baton Rouge, my coach called me into the office. His voice sounded somewhat concerned.

"Steve, I've got some bad news. A number of the conference coaches got together and ratified a significant rules change. For the first time in history, they are requiring all milers to run a qualifying heat," he said. I shook my head at the news.

"In fact, I'd call it the Stephen Bolt rule. These other coaches know about your skills, Stephen, and particularly during the indoor track season, you store a lot of team points," Coach said. That was true. I was favored in not only the mile, but also the two-mile. And since I was anchor for the two-mile relay team, we were also a threat. With this new wrinkle, they planned to force me to either pass on all the events except the mile, or so tire me out that I wouldn't be as effective.

Coach looked at me and said, "Stephen, I can't let you drop out of any races. My job is to score points for the University of Alabama, and I need you to help me score those points."

His words rang with truth. While track and field is an individual sport, in the final analysis, through the team points, the competition was school against school. Because I was a full scholarship athlete, my task was clear—to score points for Alabama. I became somewhat despondent and decided to give my best, anyway. But deep inside, I felt like my once-in-a-lifetime opportunity was stolen away from me.

As the meet progressed, I won the races I was supposed to and, on Friday night, qualified for the Saturday morning mile. The next morning, I got up early and went to the track. I felt stiff and sore physically, and a bit depressed emotionally. For the last seven years I had been running competitively and specifically for this goal. I enjoyed being goal-oriented and was generally successful. After I won that first Turkey Trot, I went on to set a series of high school records (which still stand twenty-five years later) for the state of Alabama, and then I achieved the fastest high-school mile in the nation during my senior year. Later, in college, I broke a variety of Southeastern Conference records—except the one I wanted. Now, with the way I was feeling, it looked like my goal was slipping from my grasp.

The track officials made the last call for the mile run. I shed my workout gear, put on my competition spikes, and walked up to the starting line. Suddenly I felt a rush of adrenaline. It shook me to the core. I began thinking, *What if I try anyway? So what if I fail?* Everyone—fans, sportswriters, television crews, coaches, other athletes— didn't expect me to win the race. They knew that I was tired. Suddenly the pressure disappeared and the unexpected became once again worth focusing on. But was it really within my grasp, or was this just a delusion?

With a new sense of confidence, I stepped on the track and waited for the starter to raise his hand in the air and pull the trigger on the starting gun. I thought, *The heck with it. I'm going for it.* When the gun cracked, I took off and led from the start. My only goal was to push ahead with all my heart. In an instant, my teammates figured out what was going on and quickly took their positions around the infield. With their hand gestures, they indicated if I was ahead or if I was behind a sub–four-minute pace. I was so focused that I quickly got ahead of my pace and almost didn't see them. As the adrenaline pumped through me, my muscles felt good, even if they were a bit tired and sore. By the time I reached the half-mile point, everyone in the stadium had joined in my excitement. The announcer indicated that if I maintained the same pace, I would break the four-minute mile. The fans cheered in excitement and stood on their feet; some of them even spilled onto the track.

Even the coaches who had created this Stephen Bolt rule stood and clapped in cadence as my feet touched the track through the three-quarter mark. I continued my record-breaking pace as the gun blasted to indicate the final lap. I pushed ahead. All my years of training, discipline, and drive fell into place for the final turn around the track. As I crossed the finished line and the AP photographer forever captured the moment on film, I turned my head to the left and saw the three digital clocks—each showing a sub–four-minute mile.

The crowd, my team, and my coach went wild. I finally achieved my goal. To this day, my hands sweat and my heart pumps as I relive that moment of finally achieving that worthy goal in athletics. After the interviews and celebration, I walked to my hotel, took a shower, and dressed for the trip home. Arriving at the team bus a few minutes early, I found myself alone, so I sat down on the curb. A light breeze blew on this beautiful February day in southern Louisiana, and I enjoyed the combination of the cool air and the sun's warm on my aching body. As I stared off into space, my mind wasn't concentrating on anything in particular. Like my body, my mind, too, was recovering from all the concentration. Then suddenly a most unexpected question lodged itself in my mind: *What next?*

WHAT NEXT?

For years my focus and goal had been singular: Break the four-minute mile. Now that I had made that milestone, I was confronted with the other side. Maybe I should try a sub–four-minute mile outdoors, or possibly I'd try to make the next Olympic team. Certainly my record indicated I could do that. Another possibility was to try other events, such as the 5,000-meter run or the 10,000-meter run or maybe a marathon. As I continued playing the question in my mind, I also considered taking some time off. Suddenly I realized that my drive and focus were gone. Once I had accomplished my goal, I had no purpose. The emptiness that swept over me was frightening.

During this period of my life, my spiritual life and physical life were separated. I was a Christian, and I knew that if I died I would go to heaven because of God's grace. Yet I had no knowledge of what it meant to live a life with Christ. At the time I only knew about death with Christ. It seemed to me that I determined goals for life and achieved fulfillment on my own and then God would meet me at the end. How wrong I was! God is not a God of death at all; God is a God of life. And He wanted to be as much a part of my life as of my death. Sadly, I had not yet seen Him that way.

People from all walks of life and professions charge ahead with discipline and passion as they attempt to accomplish great feats. Yet like my four-minute mile, their accomplishments are hollow when they lack a foundation in Christ, the God of life.

The New Testament includes a major public teaching from Jesus—the Sermon on the Mount. In the final words of that message, Jesus talked about the importance of foundation. When you read these words, think about your own life foundation:

"Therefore everyone who hears these words of mine and puts them into practice is like a wise man who built his house on the rock. The rain came down, the streams rose, and the winds blew and beat against that house; yet it did not fall, because it had its foundation on the rock. But everyone who hears these words of mine and does not put them into practice is like a foolish man who built his house on sand. The rain came down, the streams rose, and the winds blew and beat against that house, and it fell with a great crash" (Matthew 7:24–27).

Is the foundation of your life built on sand or rock? We each have our own individual trials and difficulties to wrestle with in this life. I am reminded of something said by Confederate General Stonewall Jackson as he looked out over what would become the field of battle at his Union opponents lined up against the background. "We have met the enemy. Either they will defeat us, or we will defeat them." That truism is certainly appropriate for military battle, but it is horribly wrong as a metaphor for life. It is impossible to defeat "the enemy" in your life. The best you can hope for is to successfully evade life's hardships, but even that is totally unrealistic. Do you know for sure that you, your family, and all your friends will live disease-free, with plenty of money, in wonderful relationships, and then die blissfully and peacefully at a ripe old age? Of course not! Those who try to dodge life's bullets end up spending all their time worrying, in anxiety, and lose life in the process.

But the great news is that you can bear up against your troubles if you have a solid foundation in Jesus. He is there for you now, tomorrow, and forever. He came that you might have rest. Truly, the battle is over and the war is won. Rest in Him, your protector and provider.

CHOOSE TO BUILD A SOLID FOUNDATION

If you don't have a solid foundation, then you can choose to build it—one day at a time. Although I usually back away from offering some universal, formulistic approach to anything, here are two fundamentals to help you begin building that foundation:

1. Throw away your preconceived ideas about religion, as Jesus suggested. Understand that your God is found in life, not laws. Get to know Him. He has invested thousands of years in weaving together His message for you.

You will find that while God created us to enjoy life and friendship with Him forever, sin broke that relationship. On our own, we tried to make ourselves acceptable to God through religion, moral living, or good works—all in vain (see Romans 3:23).

Jesus Christ is the only solution to our broken relationship with the Father. There is none other, so stop looking elsewhere. God made Himself man in the form of Jesus, so that He could become, for us, the perfect sacrifice and restore our relationship with God (see Romans 5:8).

Although you may come to appreciate what Christ did for you on an intellectual basis, as I did, until you live in Him spiritually, you will never live in His peace, confidence, and joy. That is what He means when He speaks of His kingdom. You are already justified by faith to spend an eternity with God. But what about your life on earth? I'm here to tell you that God has made provision for that, too. The joy of life with God does not start at death. It starts now!

Unless you appreciate your inadequacy without Christ and admit your sinful and broken relationship, you will still be on your own. Pride caused the first sin, and pride will do the same to you (see Romans 10:9).

2. Learn to live in Christ, to be in His will, to give all your cares to Him. If you are a believer in Christ, you have the beginnings of a solid foundation. The only thing you're missing is joy! Remove your burdens and put them at His feet. Ask Him to fill you, to lead you, to make your will into His will.

Read your Bible and learn more about Christ. Select a contemporary translation such as the *New Living Translation* or the *New International Version*.

Talk with God through prayer every day. Imagine. The God of the universe wants *you* to talk with *Him!*

Find another Christian or two who can pray with you and with whom you can regularly share your successes or challenges.

Worship and serve with other Christians in a local church where Christ is preached—joyfully!

Many people are headed on a crash course to destruction—not out of stubbornness, but out of thoughtlessness. A portion of our responsibility as believers is to help others stop and think about the purpose of their lives. Are you ignoring the meaning of Christ as it applies to your everyday life? Are you aware of the aimlessness of not considering your overall purpose day in, day out? The results of such aimless wandering affect more than your money. God gives perspective, meaning, and purpose to your life. God is the center. There is no other.

How is your life different when God is the center of your focus? Several years ago, while I served a Lutheran financial services company, I met an older woman from Colorado who did not have a great deal of money. For decades her husband had been a leading pastor in the area. I never had the opportunity to meet him, since he had died a few years before I arrived in the area. Over some tea in her living room one day, I asked her, "What is important to you?"

With a slight pause, she began to talk about her four sons. Three of them were doing quite well—in fact, two were pastors. The fourth son was forty years old and had the IQ of about a ten-year-old. He could dress himself, pack a lunch, then walk to a minimum-paying job. This youngest son lived with her. "What will happen to him when I die?" she asked. At the time she was in her mid-seventies, and she wondered about the future for her son. Her income came primarily from a fixed church pension plus a little bit of savings.

I left that session and wrestled with the possibilities. Finally I had an idea that I presented. She could transfer part of her savings into a cash value life insurance policy. At that time, interests rates were around 11% on the life insurance. If she needed the funds, she could access the money at a reasonable rate of return. If she died, an amount seven times her original investment would be paid to her beneficiaries. She liked my proposal and decided to leverage her money for the benefit of her son. At that time of her life, her life plan was to provide for her youngest son.

She died about three years later. An overflow crowd attended her funeral, and speakers were set up outside the church. Many people wanted to pay tribute to her life and the ministry of her husband. Afterward, the three prosperous children sought me out to shake my hand and thank me for my work to create a safe financial haven for their younger brother. This mother's life in Christ meant she cared for the people that she left behind—especially the son who couldn't care for himself.

Early in my financial planning practice in Nashville, a young couple came into my office. They were enthusiastic about their goals and wanted to develop a financial plan to support them. Their goals were ambitious by most standards. The husband was in medical school, and the wife was pregnant. They wanted to save enough money so that she could stay home with children and, in ten years, he could quit a paying job and the two of them could go abroad to serve as medical missionaries. We rolled up our sleeves and went to work.

The financial plan required to integrate each piece of their evolving situation so they could amass sufficient resources to allow them to achieve their goals was complex. But it was also one of the most worthwhile endeavors of my career. The relevant point here was not that they were "sacrificing" for God and looking to become missionary martyrs. Rather, it was that *they had first things first.* They knew who they were in Christ, and from that appreciation they were able to develop goals that were worthy of committing to. And only then did they require a financial plan.

Where are you right now in your foundation? Are you living life in alignment with who you are in Christ? Or are you living life by happenstance, just trying to get by? One way to begin to find alignment is through a personal inventory. Ask yourself the following questions:

- Is your current job the one that you want for the rest of your life? If not, then for how long?
- Does this occupation make the best use of your talents? Your interests?
- Do you live in the most appropriate region of the country?
- Does the area offer a solid, Bible-based church?
- Does the area fill your desire in terms of recreational activities?

- Is the climate of the area what you desire?
- Does the area offer the types of relationships, values, and culture you want?

If the answer to any of the preceding questions is no, then I recommend that you begin a process that will ultimately allow you to answer all these questions affirmatively, even if it takes you a few years to do it. The answers to these questions are often neither clear-cut nor simple; they may involve a series of moves and decisions.

One of my friends, Dr. Tom King, directed a group of Christian counselors at Two Rivers Baptist Church in Nashville, Tennessee—one of the largest in the city. His wife, Cindy, had a growing interior-design business. As Tom evaluated his life purpose and goals, he felt strongly that his children needed to be raised where the family had its roots, in a rural town in Texas. As the Kings talked about it, they decided to make the move, even though it would involve some considerable transition. It meant that they would both have to start again in their careers. Ultimately, though, the importance of their life purpose and the welfare of their children were overriding factors. Tom had a peace from Christ. Tom knew that the difficulty of the changes was a small price to pay for living his life in Christ and on purpose.

Choices in life involve compromise. The key is to intentionally consider life goals. Choose to integrate your life of faith with your physical life, thereby giving meaning, purpose, and direction to who you are. Don't segregate who you are in Christ with how you live your life.

The critical issue is to choose, to be proactive. Choosing is the difference between living and existing. Live! Enjoy and be at peace.

A number of programs are available that help you take a personal inventory and offer suggestions on life choices. Here are a couple of programs that I recommend:

- The Inventure Group, 8500 Normandale Lake Boulevard, Suite 1750, Minneapolis, MN 55437. Telephone: 612-921-8686. Fax: 612-921-8690. Email: <info@inventuregroup.com>. I've taken several of the Inventure Group's seminars. The Inventure Group is committed to igniting the spirit of discovery in individuals and in teams. They design and facilitate programs that guide people in defining and honing their talents, values, purpose, and overall natural potential. Their Web site is <www.inventuregroup.com>.

- Another organization with excellent information about life planning is New Life Ministries, PO Box 650500, Dallas, TX 75265-0500. Telephone: 1-800-NEW-HOPE. Their Web site is <www.newlife.com>.

Either one of these organizations can help you focus in a way that will lead to the development of a life plan.

After a recent financial planning seminar, a woman buttonholed me with a question. "Tell me where to put my money, Stephen," she began.

Immediately I held up my hand in protest. "I don't know anything about you."

She raced on in the conversation, "I'm forty-two years old, and I have one daughter who is now married. I have spent the last fifteen years working so that I could be debt-free. Right now the only debt I have is my mortgage and it will be paid off in another year." I looked at her, realizing that this well-meaning lady had lost her life in the process of following someone's official-sounding financial planning prescription, and she didn't even realize it. She got financial planning (in this case, getting out of debt) mixed up with life planning.

"What do you want to do with your life?" I asked. Confusion filled her face. She was totally caught off guard. I continued. "In order for me to help you determine the best use of your money, I first need to know what kind of life purpose that money will be supporting."

Sadly, she responded, "I've never thought about that. I don't know."

Life. Purpose. Plan. Money. That is the correct order.

Your money is valuable only to the extent that it serves your life purpose. This sounds so intuitive, so simple. Yet, surprisingly, most people fall into the trap of living a life of servitude to money as they unthinkingly misorder their priorities—money, plan, purpose, life. Unfortunately, because there is neither an end to nor a purpose in money itself, a financial plan arranged in this wrong order never gets past the money part. And it is not life at all.

CHAPTER 2

Myths Among Christians
About Financial Planning

"Look! There He is! Jesus Christ is right here with us! Oh, my God, this is amazing…"

I looked hard, staring into my television set, as the on-site cameras focused on a twenty-foot-by-twenty-foot air vent inside a nondescript worship sanctuary. All I saw was, well, an air vent. Apparently that's all most people saw, though there were some who seemed to be so caught up in the excitement that their eyes saw whatever their adrenaline-charged mind had imagined.

The scene was surreal. I had been channel surfing and was watching a few minutes of what had been an average worship service, when all a sudden it turned into something that you would expect from a *Ripley's Believe-It-or-Not* cartoon. It took a few minutes for Jesus to pull His face off the air vent and allow the church to return from pandemonium to reverent worship, but that was enough for me.

Christians seem to be the most gullible people on earth. The inexplicable need to satisfy the urge for supernatural bleeds into just about every aspect of Christian thought. It is nowhere more evident than in the world of financial planning and investing. Among Christians, there are numerous myths related to financial planning. Some myths simply reflect a lack of intellectual depth. Other myths, more damaging, are propounded by prominent individuals within the Christian community who spread them across the church and throughout the denominations. Individual careers are founded on these myths, and, sadly, millions of lives are adversely impacted. On the surface, these well-known public figures appear knowledgeable. But such knowledge often is simply an assumption spun from their fame, not unlike the proverbial emperor's clothes. In the course of this chapter I will correct some of the most popular misconceptions and help you find ways to test whether the emperor who seeks your deference is opulently adorned or is stark-naked.

First Myth: You Have to Understand Everything About Your Investment

There are many things with significant application that you do not understand. For example, if you have a tonsillectomy, an appendectomy, a C-section, or other medical procedure, you would most certainly have a need for enough information about the procedure to know that it makes sense for your prescription. But you would not have to know all the details, such as the types of instruments that will be used or the step-by-step intricacies of the surgery. As a patient, it's sufficient for you to understand the risks involved in the procedure, have confidence in the medical team, and then allow them to do their work.

For another example, how many of us understand what happens when we sit behind a steering wheel of a car, turn the ignition, and then drive that car down the road? I used to understand every tiny piece of the mechanical puzzle when I was in high school, but today's vehicles operate with the latest computer technology. I purchased a new car a year ago. One day I realized that I had never even lifted the hood and looked inside. Anymore, it really doesn't matter to the driver what it looks like under the hood. The degree of complexity of today's engines and transmissions vastly outstrips my ability to play home mechanic. If something goes wrong, I take it to a professional.

The same principle that is true for surgery and car repair is true for today's financial planning strategies and investment opportunities. To benefit from today's financial services you'd better hope that your financial expertise is sufficient to develop and manage your financial plan. Every aspect of your plan needs to make sense to you, but you don't need to have expert understanding of every sentence of every prospectus before you make a wise, intelligent investment decision.

Do you really need to know precisely how the transfer agent provides financial data to your chosen fund before you are comfortable? Is it really key to your ability to make a wise investment decision that you know what triggers a mutual fund manager to buy a stock? The complexity of financial instruments is such that it is virtually impossible for you to know the details of every investment category.

In fact, I recently heard a twenty-five-year industry veteran, an investment manager who controls over $150 million in assets, say, "I wouldn't know a variable annuity if it reached up and bit me in the rear." If successful financial services professionals feel free to make such comments, what does that say for the ability of the layperson?

You *do* need to understand what risks are involved and feel comfortable with them. You *do* need to understand how any particular investment fits into your portfolio, how it dovetails with your other financial instruments, and how it helps you reach your objectives. But you do *not* have to understand the various internal dynamics of the program, unless, of course, you want to.

Using the transportation example as a metaphor, in the final analysis, the choice is yours: (a) a turbo-charged, state-of-the-art refined automobile, or (b) a bicycle. If you truly believe that it is essential for you to fully understand the intricacies of every financial instrument in order to make a wise decision, you'll end up riding a bicycle through life. Your financial plan will necessarily have to be reduced to the simplest of strategies.

SECOND MYTH: CHRISTIANS SHOULD ALWAYS LOOK FOR 'GOOD DEALS'

The people who believe this believe that living life through penny-pinching increases favor with God. This tightwad undercurrent has led to many financial perils in the Christian community. One such peril was a medical-insurance scam. A recent issue of the *Wall Street Journal* reported a health insurance scam that was started by and promoted by a group of Christians. These people preyed on Christians who didn't believe in paying the market cost of health insurance premiums. The scammers' plan was to enroll Christian families and allow them to pay whatever premium they felt "led" to pay. The house of cards began tumbling down when the families tried to use their health insurance, only to discover that they actually had none.

Within the insurance business, there is an objective price for all services and material goods. This price is, of course, established by the market (albeit with increasing government manipulation). Since this so-called Christian insurance company wasn't receiving the proper premium for the actual cost of these services, there simply wasn't enough money when it came time to buy them on behalf of the insured. The old axiom—if it sounds too good to be true, then it probably *is* too good to be true—applies here. Once you suspend critical thinking in favor of looking for the best deal, greed will invite all kinds of unnecessary complications in your life. Some people believe if it costs less, it must be more Christian. This kind of thinking does not spring from a wholesome relationship with God the Father. Rather, it emanates from a sinful inner greed and pride. Including a consideration of pricing in the decision-making process is certainly prudent; subordinating all other considerations, however, is not.

THIRD MYTH: CHRISTIANS SHOULD REFRAIN FROM INVESTMENT RISK

Proponents of this myth falsely believe that to the extent they reduce investment risk, they will increase God's pleasure and their portfolio will be "blessed." The fact is, all investments hold some form of risk. It's impossible to eliminate all risk. It is both possible and prudent, however, to *lessen* your risk through a properly and well-managed investment program. Don't let concern for risk paralyze you. It is possible to make some mistakes along the way and still come out better than if you had chosen what appeared to be the safe alternative.

Consider the following hypothetical comparison between Peter, the more aggressive investor, and Thomas, who is more concerned with safety than anything else. They both plan to retire in twenty years, and they both need to accumulate $500,000 within that time in order to retire comfortably. In our comparison, we'll assume each of them begins with $100,000 in retirement savings.

Peter decided to split his $100,000 equally. He invested $25,000 into four different investments, each with varying degrees of risk. After twenty years, those investments achieved the following results:

One investment failed completely, and he lost all his money.

One investment achieved only a 3% average rate of return.

One investment achieved an 8% rate of return.

One investment achieved a 15% rate of return.

The sum total of all investments is $570,840. His wife and family should congratulate Peter, because he will now enter retirement having met his goal. Keep in mind that he did this even though he actually lost 25% of his money.

Thomas, on the other hand, was skeptical and decided to put all his money into a "safe" investment. He didn't want to be exposed to market risk, business risk, liquidity risk, or financial risk. He selected a certificate of deposit (CD) because it offered guaranteed returns. Over the twenty-year period, it returned an average of 6.5%. At the end of the period, his investment was worth $352,000, a full $148,000 short of his goal! Thomas succeeded in his desire to not lose any money, but in the process he dug himself a retirement income deficit that will forever alter his lifestyle, and that of his wife and family, too!

As Christians we are not called to gravitate toward riskless investing or to take the most conservative approach. Rather, we are called to be good stewards of all our resources, all our needs, and all our opportunities. Instead of focusing on being riskless in our investing, we should strive to take the most prudent approach within the context of our goals.

In Matthew 25, Jesus told the parable of the talents. A man was going on a long journey so he called together three servants. To the first servant, he gave five talents, to the second servant, two talents, and to the third servant, he gave one talent. The first servant put his five talents to work and gained five more. The second servant also worked with his two talents and earned two more.

Jesus shared the parable to pointedly tell about the man with only one talent. This servant dug a hole and buried his talent in the ground. When the master returned, he praised the first two servants and gave them increased responsibility. And what about the third servant who buried his talent?

He came to his master and said, "'I knew that you are a hard man, harvesting where you have not sown and gathering where you have not scattered seed. So I was afraid and went out and hid your talent in the ground. See, here is what belongs to you.'

"His master replied, 'You wicked, lazy servant! So you knew that I harvest where I have not sown and gather where I have not scattered seed? Well then, you should have put my money on deposit with the bankers, so that when I returned I would have received it back with interest. Take the talent from him and give it to the one who has the ten talents" (Matthew 25:24–28).

Then Jesus told us what the result would be if we don't use our talents. He said, "For everyone who has will be given more, and he will have an abundance. Whoever does not have, even what he has will be taken from him. And throw that worthless servant outside, into the darkness, where there will be weeping and gnashing of teeth" (Matthew 25:29–30).

The message is a pointed one for us as we consider our attitude about financial risk. The first principle in stewardship is to remember that in the final analysis, whatever money you have is not really yours. So to the extent that your interest is only in gaining from it that which will serve only you and your interests, your riskless philosophy of investing begins to again look a lot like greed. Receive the money God entrusts to you gratefully, use it for your needs, but realize it is really given to you to grow way beyond just you.

FOURTH MYTH: THE BIBLE IS AN ECONOMIC TEXTBOOK

You'll never hear it articulated exactly that way, but if you listen carefully, that's what many Christian financial "experts" are really saying. This myth needs to be solidly debunked. All too often financial planners, who do not know enough about their business, create an alternative way to convince people to do business with them. In the Christian community, the easy way is to evoke the Bible in place of prudent and sound financial advice. The Bible wasn't written as an economic textbook, any more than it was inspired to be a textbook on proper farming or medical advice. It was written to be the very Word of God that leads to salvation. If we reduce the Scriptures to that of a prescription for every financial woe, then we trivialize the Word of God.

A case in point would be the popular idea that Christians should never go into debt, and that if they do, they should get out of it as quickly as possible. For scriptural verification of this philosophy, which has created millions in personal wealth for its proponents, these misguided financial preachers quickly turn to their concordance to find any reference to debt. They find passages that discuss debt in a negative tone, and then they conveniently dissect the passages from their context and quote them. The passages are also quickly divorced from any context that offers them no profit, such as a discussion of having multiple wives, repaying a wrongdoing with an eye for an eye, and slaughtering an enemy and returning with their spoils. We don't hear much preaching in favor of multiple wives, revenge, and plundering our enemies because we all recognize that such preaching would be a blatant misappropriation of the Word of God. The fact that the misappropriation of Scripture deals with something benign like debt instead of something hideous like the wholesale pillage of a nation makes the misappropriation no less wrong.

Of course debt can be wrong. And misuse of credit can create immense problems capable of wreaking havoc for many years. But such can also be said about wealth, or anything else, for that matter. The key word to focus on is not *debt,* but *misuse.* And focusing so much on staying out of debt that you fail to buy the car when you need it or that you fail to accept the responsibility for a mortgage on a home that your family needs can also be a misuse of debt. Looking again at the example from Matthew, the master demanded that his servant should have at least put the money in the bank where it would have gained interest. This demand indicated that Jesus well understood that borrowing and bank interest play very real parts in the financial equation.

I recommend that Christians steer clear of financial preachers who quote Scripture to dictate specific decisions for the development and management of financial planning.

CHAPTER 3

Why Use a
Financial Planner?

The Advantages of Using a Financial Planner

Why use a financial planner? What are the advantages? There are several reasons why you may want to use a financial planner.

COMPREHENSIVE FINANCIAL PLANNING SOFTWARE

First, you turn to a professional in the financial area because a planner has access to a sophisticated and comprehensive financial planning information from three different dimensions of a personal information questionnaire. Through complex mathematical computations, the report shows the planner what kinds of things the person will need to change about the present allocation of financial resources to accomplish the future financial goals.

For example, let's say you want to retire at age sixty-five with an income of $3,400 a month. But after calculating your various assets, their current funding levels, and projected rates of return, it appears that you are going to be short of reaching your goal. One of the reasons has to do with the impact of inflation, historically at around 3.5% a year. So, at age sixty-five, the $3,400 becomes $7,748 in inflated dollars. When you fall short of your goal you are presented with two options: Either you can (a) increase your rate of return on your current investments, or (b) you can increase the amount of your contribution to the investments. If we assume that you don't have any additional money that you could use to supplement your monthly investing, that means you'll have to increase the rate of return on your investments.

After looking over your Investment Risk Profile, your planner determines that you are a fairly conservative investor who can't handle more than a 5% to 10% swing in your return. You say, "Yes, that's right." You might even turn to your spouse and ask, "Honey, what do you think?"

She raises up in her chair with an indignant attitude, "No, I'm not comfortable with a 5% to 10% loss to my principal. Are you actually talking about losing money? I'm not going to lose money." With this response, if I were the planner, I would know that I have my work cut out for me, because you can't get there with the financial resources, risk profile, and attitude they have. The math just doesn't work.

Then I might say, "OK. But without taking some amount of risk, we're going to have to construct a very conservative portfolio with a return expectation of only somewhere in the 5% to 10% range."

You glance up and say, "OK."

I continue, "Well, because you want to retire at age sixty-five with $3,400 a month of inflation adjusted income, you don't have any additional money to invest, and you will not agree to a slightly higher volatility level of investing, then we have only one option left. You will have to wait to retire... about nine years."

"No, we can't," they both say in unison. "We've been planning our retirement for a long time. We don't know when our health may fail, and we have to be able to retire at sixty-five!"

These clients have unrealistically negative perceptions about risk, given their investment time frame. They can handle a greater swing in their portfolio, probably as high as a 15% swing. What they need more than anything is education—education about tough choices, risk management, and financial planning. Left without this education, many people will take the starvation approach to investing and money management. A financial planner has access to state-of-the-art technology that indicates clearly what the issues are, so that solutions to the tough choices involved in accomplishing life goals can be found.

EXPERTISE OF FINANCIAL PLANNER

Second, you utilize a financial planner because of his or her expertise. A qualified planner should know a great deal of information that the clients don't know and cannot access. The planner should be able to devise creative solutions that benefit the clients in ways better than they could create with their own resources.

Many clients, for example, make a pivotal mistake. They believe that if their investments are divided among two to five different mutual funds that they are adequately diversified. However, statistics show that in order to reduce overall portfolio volatility, investors should opt for more than an arbitrary allocation of money over different mutual funds. They also need a proper asset allocation, that is, having their money invested in several asset classes such as U.S. stocks, small company stocks, international bonds, corporate bonds, and natural resources. These various asset classes should be somewhat negatively correlated with each other so that when one of the asset classes suffers a market decline in its value, then another asset class in the same investment portfolio might be gaining. Over time, the end result will be solid returns accompanied with lower overall volatility.

The academic body of knowledge supporting this technology of portfolio management has won two Nobel prizes in economic science and is employed by most of the world's pension plan managers. Without an expensive and highly sophisticated software program, continuously updated, coupled with a high degree of portfolio management competency, you will not be able to construct and manage this type of portfolio.

SPECIALIZED WORLD

Third, you should take advantage of a financial professional because today's world has become specialized. No consumer (no matter how sophisticated or well read) can become familiar with all the variety of financial instruments sold today. Nor can the consumer distinguish the benefits and disadvantages of each investment opportunity and then prudently determine how much to invest and over what period of time. It's certainly possible for an individual to develop a do-it-yourself financial plan. However, by definition that plan will be dumbed down to the individual's level of expertise and resource accessibility. (Remember the bicycle metaphor we discussed earlier.) Competent financial advice is similar to other professional advice and services, such as medical, legal, or accounting. The fact is, most often the results obtained on your own will not approach the benefits of having utilized the services of a competent professional.

PROFESSIONAL DISCIPLINE

Fourth, if you are like most humans, you lack the discipline to stay the course of your financial plan without a professional's help. When we have a financial crisis, our conviction to develop a financial plan grows. Then, after the crisis subsides, we revert to our normal life—the kids have soccer practice, the muffler on the car needs replacement, the house needs repainting, the grandparents visit for summer vacation. In the meantime, our financial plan begins to lose its sense of urgency.

One of my financial planner friends in Canada says, "If you have a problem, turn it into a procedure and you won't have that problem any more." If you lack a systematic plan to meet your financial needs and wants, the procedure is to locate a professional financial planner to manage the process.

Beyond the Myths—Developing a Financial Plan

Mirrors. Some people love them. These are the people who touch their hair every time they walk past one. Other people don't like what they see and rush past any mirror that confronts them. Once you have the peace, confidence, and joy that follows a true appreciation of who you are in Christ, then you're ready to take the next step—an honest look in the mirror and an assessment of your current life plan. Without that look in the mirror, you are not operating with full information.

A couple from Hermitage, Tennessee, came to see me. As we talked, I learned they were in their late fifties and facing retirement in about four years. Over the years, they had never had a relationship with a financial planner. As they considered retirement, they understood that the move from the accumulation phase of life to the distribution phase would require some professional help. At this point in time, they needed to consider their investments within the context of life expectancy, integrating considerations of risk, return, and taxes. So the couple filled out the Personal Information Form and we began the process of analyzing their current financial picture.

In a subsequent meeting, I presented them with some tough choices. Based on their Investment Risk Profile, I knew they didn't like anything invested in the stock market. I explained, "Based on what you are telling me, you will have to think about reducing your expectations for retirement income. You will not be able to live as you dreamed about, or in a manner you had been anticipating."

For about an hour, we talked about these issues and how their choices will impact their retirement dreams. They didn't like any of the possibilities. Armed with the information, they took it home to think about. One of my suggestions was to move half of their retirement assets into market-based investments (which would fluctuate in value). They didn't like that suggestion, but they also had a great dislike for the looming possibility of having to change their lifestyle. Their current investments were in certificates of deposit (CDs), savings accounts, and fixed annuities.

At their next appointment, the couple wanted to learn more about this market-based investment approach. I explained the concept of investing in the market using a strategy referred to as asset allocation. Simplified, such a strategy would allocate portions of their money into several different classes or categories of investments on a diversified basis. We would invest in different sized companies, different industries, some stocks, some bonds, and even different countries, as I made reference to in the earlier example. The body of academic research support-ing this strategy is called Modern Portfolio Theory (MPT). Using this science, it's the least risky method of entering the market. After a long discussion, they were willing to take the plunge so they could attempt to preserve their current lifestyle.

Unfortunately, I gave this advice in late 1993, when the markets had been good. Although I rarely talked about what happened in the markets over the recent months because of its historic irrelevancy in the long run, these clients were well aware of the above-average returns for the past year. However, then in 1994, the Federal Reserve did something unprecedented. Five times in that year, they raised the interest rates—which is the death knell for the market. Over those twelve months, the market performed very poorly. Now I had put 50% of this couple's retirement assets into market-based investments. Throughout the year, the couple came into the office with long faces that reflected their anxiety and discouragement. I kept saying, "Hang in there. Trust the science. Trust the math and the history." During that first year, I did a lot of handholding.

The second year, they had good returns—in fact excellent. The third and fourth years were also excellent. In fact, so good were the returns that their confidence in the markets grew roots. Then, during one of our annual reviews, these people, so risk-averse that they almost opted for a pittance in retirement income over having to accept market risk, actually asked me, "Can we move *all* our money into the market?"

Today almost all their retirement funds have been reallocated from fixed instruments to market-based investments. Their portfolio has grown so much that what began small is now large. Even if they lose 15% of the large sum, they still have much more profit than they ever would have had in the fixed market. But it was tough going the first year as this couple considered a new approach to investing. The learning process for them, as with most people, wasn't instantaneous.

The first prudent decision this couple made was to look into the mirror. What they initially saw reflected made them quite uncomfortable. The next positive step they took was to seek professional assistance. After making appropriate changes, they no longer feared looking into the mirror. We'll discuss more about mirrors—the financial planning process—later. But first, let's qualify the professional help that may be needed.

Choosing the Right Financial Planner

A financial planner is the qualified professional who can help you appropriate your financial resources in a way that will support your life goals. This person might be young, old, male, or female. You need to spend a serious amount of time interviewing financial planners. You may only need to interview from two to four planners to choose the appropriate one for you. Interview a variety of planners so that you have a taste of the various personality types, styles of practice, and fee schedules.

There is plenty of room for varying personalities and styles, but there are also certain fundamentals that should always be there. Let's review some of them.

FULL-TIME PROFESSIONAL

A qualified financial planner must be engaged in the business full-time, not part-time. Preferably, he is also associated with a firm of other professionals. Then, if necessary, he can call on others for additional assistance in areas of their specialty.

You might find it helpful to have a prepared list of questions when interviewing financial planners. These questions could include:

- How long have you been practicing this profession?

- What type of success have you achieved?

- How many clients do you have? I would be hesitant to work with someone who had fewer than fifty clients. However, if the median client profile is $2 million of net worth, then it might be reasonable for that particular financial planner to only have twenty-five clients.

- What does the median client profile look like? You would want that profile to describe you.

- What licenses do you hold? The National Association of Security Dealers (NASD) licenses individuals to transact business in the U.S. Registration is not optional; the law requires it. The process involves written examinations and continuing education. Also the planner should have a life insurance and a health insurance license.

- What professional designations do you have? Financial planning requires competency in a wide range of subdisciplines including investments, insurance, estate planning, and income taxation.

The College of Financial Planning in Denver, Colorado, is the only independent academic institution with the purpose of certifying financial planners. Under the operation of the National Endowment for Financial Education (NEFE), the college has established a rigorous curriculum to test for competency in each area of financial planning: insurance and risk management, investment planning, income taxes, retirement planning, and estate planning.

After each quarter of study, the candidate takes a test. When a candidate has successfully passed each area of study, then he or she completes a two-day, ten-hour comprehensive examination. This test is demanding. The last time I checked, the pass rate for the examination was only 52%. Certification for a candidate is achieved only after successful completion of the examinations, a personal background check from the college and achievement of a level of vocational experience.

When a candidate has fulfilled these requirements, he is granted the status of Certified Financial Planner (CFP). Because of the rigorous educational curriculum, as well as the academic integrity of the entire program, I recommend this license as the best starting point when you begin looking for professional financial assistance. I am not a big fan of a lot of what the College for Financial Planning does beyond administering a rigorous curriculum, but I am an advocate of their academic integrity.

While there are other license designations such as ChFC (Chartered Financial Consultant) or CLU (Chartered Life Underwriter) or LUTC (Life Underwriters Training Council), in my opinion, these licenses are not as comprehensive or intellectually demanding as a CFP. There are probably a dozen other designations that you'll see on financial planners' business cards, but most of these are more along the order of belonging to a trade association than reflective of academic achievement. Also, these other designations may be biased toward the life insurance industry.

Keep in mind that attorneys and accountants are not financial planners. Unfortunately, most of them will jump at the chance to give you their opinions on the subject, but they have neither academic training nor experience in the field to back their opinions.

BUSINESS ENVIRONMENT

Who is actually going to process the business? Does the planner have a staff? Is the planner a one-person shop? Does he meet you in your home, or does he have an office? If a planner is doing a good job for his clients, then he will need staff support. The financial planning business is extremely management intensive. You don't want your planner spending his or her time doing paperwork, filing, and keeping up with administrative details. Instead, you want the planner thinking creatively and learning about new and better planning strategies.

It's acceptable for a planner to work in his or her home—but it's preferable for the planner to have a separate office. The outside office space is another concrete measure of the client base and the planner's commitment to service his clients in a professional manner. It shows your planner is willing to spend several thousand dollars each month to develop a professional presence and transact business in a professional way.

In most cases, the highly regulated securities industry strictly prohibits representatives from recommending any product not offered through the broker-dealer that he represents. This can limit the scope of a planner's capacity to meet your needs, particularly if the broker-dealer is associated with an insurance company, or is small. I advise finding a professional who is associated with an independent broker-dealer that offers insurance and investments from hundreds of different product sponsors. This way the professional can offer multiple options in all the mainstream financial product categories. Then you can gain the benefit of his firm's research into the various competing products in the marketplace.

CHEMISTRY

This qualification for a planner is less tangible, but it is an absolutely necessary part of the selection process. Otherwise the relationship is doomed to failure. The chemistry has to go both directions. Not only does the client have to enjoy the planner, but also the planner must want to work with the client. On occasion, I have turned away potential clients simply because the chemistry didn't work.

About four years ago, an older woman telephoned and said, "My husband and I are interviewing financial planners. My husband is about seventy years old, and we need some assistance. We'd like to make an appointment to see you."

When I met the couple, the husband looked very stern and cold. I tried to be warm and develop some chemistry and common ground for discussion. But this man wanted nothing to do with it. He positioned me at the head of the table, then pointed to my right for his wife to sit, and then he sat at my left. He got out three typed, single-spaced sheets of paper that listed his assets and placed a copy in front of each of us.

For the next twenty minutes, he read the list and justified why each asset in his portfolio had been purchased. Then he looked at me and said, "Today I'm here to find out from you what you would change and why."

Immediately I could tell the relationship was not going to work. This man didn't want my counsel; he was looking for an argument. And even if I "won" on this day, it would continue for years to come. My guess is that this argumentative, combative style was formed as a part of his personality many years ago. With my kindest effort, I worked my way out of the situation. I terminated the meeting saying, "I wish you well in your search for a financial planner." The man, who had a net worth of over $1 million, looked shocked. Nonetheless, I had no interest in taking on that kind of client, regardless of how much money he had.

The lack of chemistry isn't always on the client side of things. I've met planners who are overbearing, arrogant, and demanding. And sometimes it goes to the other extreme, where they are so timid that you never receive any substance from them.

EDUCATION

It's important to understand that bankers, attorneys and Certified Public Accountants (CPAs) are not financial planners. While their professions can be important to the financial planning process, they are not specifically equipped to assist you with your financial goals. Most bankers have almost no formal education in financial planning. Attorneys are required to take only a few hours of education in estate planning to become a member of their bar. And CPAs are accountants, not financial planners. CPAs do audits and tax returns or assist with business plans, but these skills do not provide them the academic base to help you develop a financial plan.

In the same line of reasoning, make sure you do not confuse intelligence with competency. A brain surgeon is highly educated in a very specific field and is likely very intelligent. However, because this doctor lacks the formal academic training in financial planning, he will be a less than competent financial advisor (whether he admits it or not!). Also make sure you don't confuse trust and love with overall competency. Your father may love you deeply and, if you request his assistance in financial planning, he may give you whatever information he has available to him, even if he's had no specific training in the field. Unfortunately, his lack of competency will eventually cause you to have a financial plan with less-than-optimum performance. If you asked for his assistance in another area—say, heart surgery—he would immediately recognize his lack of competency and, motivated by love, refer you to a qualified heart surgeon (unless of course, he is a heart surgeon). You should exercise equal common sense in the area of financial planning.

As pointed out earlier, the financial planner should be competent and familiar with a wide range of such financial-planning subdisciplines as investments, insurance, income taxes, and estate planning. What happens when you don't deal with a financial planner who is well versed on these subdisciplines? Your financial plan can become self-defeating. A couple of years ago I witnessed an example of this. Many people mistakenly believe that if someone has a high profile and makes a lot of money that he has excellent advisors. This assumption isn't necessarily true, and, in many cases, it's exactly the opposite.

A high-profile, instantly recognized sports figure who was a client of mine had a net worth of about $7 million and an income of about $1 million each year. This man had been receiving advice from a stockbroker who knew nothing about insurance or income taxes or estate planning. When this client came to me, I discovered he was paying profoundly high income taxes because no one had introduced him to tax-saving strategies. For every $1 million of income, he gave up $450,000 in taxes. I suggested a few alterations in his investing strategy that resulted in his next $1 million of income being taxed at only 20%. That's a saving of $250,000 in one year because of proper financial advice.

As we worked with this client, we found he had paid about $2,500 for estate planning advice that included a living trust and a life insurance trust. The fact that no one bothered to follow up and move the client's assets into the trusts meant that they were virtually worthless.

Unless corrected, it appeared the family would pay an additional $1.6 million in federal estate taxes.

In the area of insurance, the stockbroker turned over all insurance-related considerations to an insurance salesman. The insurance salesman buttonholed this high-profile client and convinced him to put $250,000 cash into a single premium whole life policy. The result of this mistake was substantial. It meant the internal rate of return on the $250,000 policy was only in the area of 2.5% to 3%! And because the insurance was not handled outside of the client's estate, it meant that as much as 55% of the death proceeds would be consumed by federal estate taxes. This decision was in no way a coordinated part of a well thought through financial plan.

From my point of view, having been an independent financial planner, this client was taken advantage of. The key broker was referring the client to other people in the company for insurance and estate planning—yet, because of his lack of competency in these fields, he had no way of making sure there was an overall coordinated strategy to all the decisions. So the insurance agent, accountants, attorneys, and the broker were all making money from the client, but the client was left spending a great deal of financial resources with little to show for it. This sports figure expected his advisor to provide competent planning, but in fact, his advisor was not competent at all, and his advice certainly did not reflect planning.

The Three Important Principles

Regardless of whether or not you choose to work with a planner who is a CFP, you, need to develop and manage a financial plan that is customized to your specific life goals. here are three principles to use in the search for professional assistance: (1) academic integrity, (2) product neutrality, and (3) plan management. The right planner will reflect these principles in his work with you.

ACADEMIC INTEGRITY

A well developed financial plan begins like a science project. It integrates various pieces into a systematic whole in order to produce an effective result. That sounds complicated, but it really isn't. To simplify the understanding, sometimes it's easier to start by eliminating what financial planning is *not*.

- Financial planning is *not* simply a budget.
- Financial planning is *not* merely the purchase of an insurance policy or annuity.
- Financial planning is *not* an account with a broker solely because he is your father's favorite broker.

Financial planning is the systematic management of your financial resources (cash, investments, retirement accounts, debts, insurance policies) toward the support of your particular life goals. You manage those resources in the most prudent manner to maximize their financial benefit as they relate to your financial goals. This process is dynamic, flexible, and evolutionary. We will discuss this principle in greater detail as it is reflected in the Comprehensive Financial Analysis.

PRODUCT NEUTRALITY

Product neutrality is the second principle related to selecting professional assistance. Let's say that you want to buy a new car. You drive into a Ford dealership and begin talking with a salesman. What brand of car do you think the salesman will recommend? A Toyota? A Chrysler? I don't think so. Yet many people solicit financial advice in the same way. They turn to a salesperson who is associated with a company that only sells proprietary products.

You might find a financial planner who is a Christian and a CFP, has all the necessary licenses, has 200 clients, and has been in the business for five years. Sounds like the perfect candidate so far. But because this hypothetical planner works as a captive agent for an insurance company, what types of products do you think he will recommend to you? Regardless of what might be most beneficial for your situation, he is constrained by the relationship with his company. He has no choice but to recommend only his company's products. Here's the critical question to ask yourself: Are these the products that you need? The problem is, you aren't really going to know. Bingo. That's why it's better if you work with an independent planner who is licensed through an independent broker-dealer.

Your financial planner should have access to a variety of investment and insurance companies. In fact, this planner should have access to virtually every type of financial instrument that could possibly be needed for a client who fits your profile. For example, the planner should be able to access multiple families of mutual funds, several insurance companies, and options for other types of programs such as tax credit programs, energy programs, limited partnerships, and a host of money managers.

PLAN MANAGEMENT

The final element of our three important principles is plan management. Plan management will allow you maximum flexibility to handle change—whether you want it or not, life will deal you many changes. And as you face changes in your life, you also want your financial plan to reflect these changes. As a minimum, you should meet with your financial planner once a year to monitor your plan. Before this meeting, your planner should update all your financial records and rerun all the analyses. Then, during your meeting, you will have the necessary information to determine if your plan needs to be changed.

Too often, both consumers and financial services professionals make the mistake of investing many hours of research and discussion in order to produce a financial plan, only to then walk away from it and never referring to it again.

When These Three Elements Are Not in Focus

Academic integrity means you'll have a complete picture of your present situation, along with the available strategies you can use to make improvements. Product neutrality means that you'll have access to financial products such as mutual funds and insurance plans from many different companies. Plan management means that you'll have continual professional oversight of your plan to make sure that any changes that are required as you move forward are appropriately integrated into your plan in the years to come. This is how the financial planning process should work in a perfect world. But our world is not perfect.

Many years ago, I was a general agent for a large insurance and investment company and had only recently become a CFP. I found myself wrestling with the issue of developing financial plans based on academic integrity.

One day I got a phone call from a registered representative (a licensed individual who sells securities) who reported to me, "I've placed a good piece of business (meaning he had made some money), but the guy is sort of going backward on his decision. Can you come down and help me?"

"Sure," I said. Then I found out the name of the client. He was a senior pastor in the city—a scholarly gentleman who had helped thousands of people in their spiritual journey. Pastors are not paid well, and now this pastor was facing retirement in three or four years with inadequate financial resources.

Jerry had recommended a particular insurance-related investment program, which was limited to four investment options. I agreed to meet with the pastor and Jerry, and I listened as Jerry went over and over the virtues of this particular investment program. As they talked, the pastor's confidence in the program increased.

But as I listened, my discomfort increased. Sitting around the pastor's dining room table, he finally took a deep breath and sighed. Then he sat back and said, "OK, I'll keep the program. But I have one more question. There are four investment options in this program. Who is going to help me figure out which ones to put my money in and decide when I need to change that allocation? You know, for how long and what percentage of my money should go into each one?"

Jerry leaned across the table and said with self-inflated pomp, "That's where I come in." Now I knew for a fact that Jerry had about as much competency in that area as anybody off the street. Six months earlier this registered representative was selling jewelry behind the counter at a major retail chain! Certainly Jerry was a Christian, but that did not give him any special investment advisor competency.

I had watched as this pastor entrusted his life savings to Jerry's management. Even under the best of circumstances with the best professional help in the world, the pastor was going to eke out a meager retirement. The least he deserved was competent, professional assistance. But he didn't get that quality professional help. He got a former jewelry salesman who had been in the industry for six months. I almost threw up at the scene, yet I was helpless to do anything about it, because there was nothing illegal about what had taken place, and the salesman had done precisely what his company had trained him to do: *Sell their products.* I walked away from that meeting more determined than ever to educate people and do something about the future of financial planning. This book is one step in that direction.

Christian Values System

Does the planner have a values system that is consistent with yours? Values shouldn't be the only consideration, but your planner's values system should be considered significant. In fact I would rank it at least as high as licenses, years in the business, number of clients, and product neutrality.

Many Christians, however, make the mistake of putting so much emphasis on shared values that they fail to properly evaluate the other key qualifications. This mistake can and does lead to a lot of frustration, havoc, and unfulfilled goals down the road. At the Values Financial Network, we have a saying, "Do business with us because of the quality of work that we do. The fact that we are Christians only enhances the relationship. It should not cause the relationship."

To illustrate this principle, consider a well-known Christian marketer who refers to himself as a financial advisor. This "expert" hosts a national radio program and has a following in the hundreds of thousands. Yet the *only criterion* which this person meets on my list of qualifications for financial planners is that he is a Christian. As a result, I have heard this marketer make numerous and substantial mistakes in his advice to people on his radio program. Because he doesn't adequately understand economics in general and financial planning specifically, he tends to present an apocalyptic vision of the economic future. In fact, his focus has most often been on telling people about the coming economic collapse and how they should prepare. Consequently, the financial decisions that people are led to by this type of advice are often stunted, shortsighted, and uncoordinated. Imagine how dramatically different your financial decisions would be if they were based on a coming apocalypse. Because this marketer isn't licensed and has no industry professional certifications such as CFP, no regulatory body holds him accountable for his off-the-wall prognostications. So, although he meets the qualification of "shared values," he does not meet any of the other critical components of a professional financial planner.

How Are Financial Planners Compensated?

If you have diligently followed the advice in the previous section, it will be hard for you to make a mistake in this area. Among financial planners, there is a huge debate over this particular issue—and it will never be resolved. Some planners prefer to charge a fee for their service and they feel strongly that to do so is the most objective approach. Other planners don't charge any fee for planning, but instead they are compensated through commissions on the sale of financial instruments. These planners feel their approach is fairer since clients are not under any obligation to pay for service unless they implement a financial plan.

FEE-ONLY FINANCIAL PLANNERS

Fee-only planners charge a fee for their time and explain that ultimate neutrality in the product area is their advantage. In other words, they won't be motivated to recommend a high commission strategy to you, since no commissions are involved. They contend that clients should opt to pay for the professional's time and expertise, which would therefore be unbiased. As a result, the clients, if they choose to do so are free to go elsewhere to implement the plan.

But this strength of neutrality is also a weakness. For a financial plan to be effective, it has to be managed for many years to come. You want to be sure that your planner has an incentive to keep up not only with the academics involved in the planning process, but also with the changing financial product side. It is difficult to rationalize that a fee-only planner would be as motivated to continuously research tax credit programs, mutual funds, investment mangers, insurance products, and all the rest of the product landscape if he received no compensation for implementing his recommendations.

According to the latest survey from the College for Financial Planning, the median cost of a financial plan is $800, but can amount to as much as $5,000. The median hourly rate is $95.*

COMMISSION-ONLY PLANNERS

Once the planner does the analysis, he makes some recommendations and then implements the plan. For example, you may have to purchase life insurance or

---

* According to CFP Annual Survey, 1997 data.

invest in mutual funds, or you might need a tax credit program. A commission is built into almost every single financial instrument. In nine times out of ten, even when you pay for "objective" advice, you will also pay a commission to implement your financial plan—whether it's to the firm that gives the advice or to another.

Let's consider the flip side of the fee-only approach. The other possibility is to use a commission-only planner whose advantage is that he works for free—in a sense. Actually he can't get paid until you buy something, which naturally increases his incentive to sell you a particular product. By definition, this planner cannot give you objective advice because if you don't really need to purchase anything, say for example life insurance, then in one sense you've taken away the planner's ability to be compensated. For this obvious reason, the commission-only type of planner is not necessarily the better choice.

MY OWN HYBRID APPROACH TO THE COMPENSATION ISSUE

About four years ago, I created a hybrid approach that serves to balance the competing interests in the financial planning process. Most of the affiliates of the Values Financial Network will use the following approach.

For my staff and me to spend an appropriate amount of considered time with clients, we have to know that no matter what decisions are made, we will be fairly compensated. We charge our clients an average fee of $400, and for this fee, the client receives a Comprehensive Financial Analysis and a Financial Organizer in a three-ring binder, and a minimum of four hours of our time. This approach allows me to pursue the process without the concern for having to make a sale. It also allows the clients to receive a comprehensive analysis that they can choose to implement through us or to take elsewhere, and at a price that is 50% of the going rate.

Is the Proximity of the Financial Planner Important?

The exact location of your financial planner relative to your residence is unimportant. I have had clients scattered all across the nation. One of my clients is in the Dallas/Fort Worth, Texas, area. We have met only twice. I've not had a meeting with them in over two years other than over the phone. It was critical to establish rapport in a face-to-face session early in the process. But from then on, we could proceed without requiring either party to travel.

My suggestion is that you locate a financial planner who works with an independent broker-dealer. The fees should be low enough to allow you to engage his services without it causing a major financial burden on you. The planner should have similar values to yours (more about this important topic later in the book), be someone you enjoy working with, and have associates that he can turn to for additional assistance.

How to Locate a Financial Planner

Call the Values Financial Network at 1-888-346-8258 to locate an affiliated financial professional in your area. We have developed an extensive network of Christian financial planners who meet the above standards of professionalism. Or you can locate the information on our Web site, <http://www.vfn.net/>. The site includes a national map that allows you to click on your individual state, where VFN affiliates will be listed in your area.

CHAPTER 4

What Does Financial
Planning Involve?

Now that you've selected your financial planner, what happens next?

The Three-Step Planning Process

At the Values Financial Network, we recommend that financial planning be done in a three-step process.

INTRODUCTION TO FINANCIAL PLANNING—THE FIRST INTERVIEW

The first session or initial interview is complimentary. I've never heard of a planner who charges for this introductory session. This session will provide you with an opportunity to know more about the planner. He is going to explain his planning process. How will it be accomplished? Will there be others on his staff whom you will interface with in this process? How much time will it require? What will it cost, and how will the fees be structured?

This is a get-acquainted session that lasts between thirty and sixty minutes. During that interview, the planner should ask why you are interested in financial planning and what specific things motivated you to do a financial plan? There may be a life event or personal issue that drives your motivation.

For example, a client may say, "I just moved into town," "I just changed jobs and got a big promotion," "I am thinking about buying a new house," or "I've received a large inheritance." Or it could be simply, "I'm not pleased with my current investment program." Any type of change in your personal life or your financial life may trigger a session with a planner. The planner will want to know about this motivation, and you should get some degree of comfort with his initial responses. You should not expect the planner to make specific recommendations—yet—but rather cover those issues in a broad conceptual manner.

At the end of the session, the planner will give you a homework assignment. You will need to complete a Personal Information Form (see Appendix I).

The financial analysis creates a complete picture. Remember the mirror? Your financial plan starts there. Don't be bashful, step right up and stare. Stare with the confidence that, regardless of your degree of comfort about what you might initially see, for the rest of your life once you've completed the process, every time you see that mirror again, you will be at peace with what is reflected.

The process needed to develop a financial analysis sounds complicated, but in reality it's straightforward. Two overriding dimensions need to be fully considered. One involves taking inventory of your financial resources; the other involves identifying your goals and objectives. As in the case of a vacation, if you fail to appropriately consider both dimensions, you'll either end up halfway through without any money, or you'll have money, but you'll not be enjoying it as you could.

The questions you'll need to address when completing the Personal Information Form require an honest look at your current financial situation. It is important to pay attention to accuracy, even if requires a bit of effort on your part to gather the necessary information.

Often we have this sort of information in a variety of places. The value of such information comes when you pull it into an integrated document for study. To help you become familiar with this process, I've included an example of this questionnaire in Appendix I.

Some of this information isn't easily located and will cause some frustration in finding it, so be prepared. Some of the information will be in your bank checkbook, but it will need to be reconstructed. Some of it may need to come from your accountant or attorney. Some may come from the benefits administration department at work. Some of it might even be gathering dust on the top of your refrigerator. Yes, one of my clients actually stuck his life insurance policy on top of the refrigerator and forgot about it. If the information isn't readily available, then figure out how to get it.

Incidentally, don't make the process any more tedious than it has to be. For example, there are no grades given on the form for penmanship. In fact, sometimes you don't have to fill in every blank if you provide supplemental materials like copies of insurance policies, account statements, and retirement-account reports. The point is to provide thorough information.

I always warn people in advance about this process. First, it isn't fun. You are not going to enjoy it, so be prepared for that from the beginning. You will have to appropriate time from your life for the purpose, probably from two to four hours. The good news, though, is that once you complete this form, you will never have to complete it again. From that point forward, it is simply a matter of updating the records.

The first portion of the process involves objective information about your current financial situation. For example, you will need to list your various assets (separately for husband, wife, and jointly held property), including:

- Retirement accounts
- Investments
- Insurance contracts
- Checking account
- Savings account

- Money Market accounts
- Personal property, including residence and automobiles

The second portion is more subjective and deals with what you want the money to do for your life. This section includes such questions as:

- When do you want to retire? What will you do during retirement?
- How much money do you want to have when you retire?
- Do you want to help your children through college? How much money do you want to give them?
- Are you planning for a second home?
- Are you planning for a change in residence?
- Do you want to set aside appropriate funds for recreation such as a boat or horses or an avocation?
- Do you have any significant gifts that you want to make? To the church? To a mission?
- Is there a period of time in your life when you would like to not work in order to serve in the mission field, or to study some subject, go to school, or help an ailing family member?
- Do you have plans to begin your own business? For you or your spouse or both?
- Are you going to have children? Do you want one spouse to stay home and, if so, for how long?

These questions are not exhaustive, but they acquaint you with some of the possibilities for consideration in this process.

As I consider how some people think about financial goals, I have a favorite saying—"Some people tiptoe through life so they can arrive at death safely." Many times Christians take this approach toward their financial planning. These people believe that since heaven is their certain destination, they should take no risks in their earthly life. This philosophy is totally contrary to Christ's teaching.

Each one of us has the freedom to pursue our own individual way through life. Goals vary in length, structure, specificity, and resources. There is no correct Christian standard for when to retire or for how much to help with your child's college education or for whether you should go into a second career. What a joy it is to live every day in the knowledge that God breathed life into us as individuals, knowing us even before we were born, and that nothing can separate us from the love of God. What a passion for life we have when we desire to live a life of purpose, reflecting God's creativity, love, and joy throughout our life plan as it evolves.

Don't be too demanding of yourself for hard and fast goals. Keep in mind that life is dynamic and that no matter what goals you establish, you will change and refine them over a period of time. The central purpose of goal setting is to establish a clear direction. Take a few moments to consider what you want to have in your future and when you want it to happen.

Your goals don't have to be singular. You can have four or five simultaneous goals—retirement, a second home, sending somebody through college, maybe taking four years off. Each of these goals might require a different time horizon and a different investment strategy. The key lies in flexibility and individualization. You should follow the plan and strategy that are right for you. One of the most critically important objectives for a financial planner is to free people from feeling the need to fit their life into someone else's preconceived idea. As the saying goes, there is no such thing as a dress rehearsal for life. This is it. The life you are living now and planning for in the future is the only one you get. So, do it *your* way, as a natural outgrowth and reflection of your relationship with God.

Mini-Marathon—the Second Interview

The second session with your planner lasts from two to two and a half hours. During this session, the planner will review the details of your financial situation with you line by line and page by page.

All the effort you put in to filling out the Personal Information Form will bear fruit in the form of a Comprehensive Financial Analysis. The Comprehensive Financial Analysis will be the basis for determining whether you are on track to reach your goals or whether you'll need to make some changes. Your financial analysis should be comprehensive and unbiased. You need to be able to see the entire picture before you can make any decisions. And you need to keep in mind that any analysis that a salesperson uses specifically to market a particular financial product (such as life insurance, annuities, or stocks) might have a bias toward this particular product built into the result.

Any Comprehensive Financial Analysis should include:

- Cash flow report
- Net worth statement
- Insurance analysis
- Income tax projection
- Investment portfolio analysis
- Retirement income projection
- Education funding report
- Estate transfer report
- Personal values analysis

As these reports are reviewed, the planner will be giving you suggestions, strategies, options, and solutions for you to consider. The session requires a great deal of interaction between you and the planner. Typically, at the end of this session you feel like the Gary Larson cartoon character who, sitting in a classroom, raises his hand and says, "Teacher, may I be excused? My brain is full." Hopefully, your planner will summarize the discussion and recommend a course of action.

One caution for this step in the process: Don't get caught up in "analysis paralysis." Fear of making a mistake can totally immobilize some people, rendering them unable to do anything. If this happens to you, remember the adage from the book *In Search of Excellence:* "Disorganized action is always preferable to organized inaction." The key is to do something.

At the end of this mini-marathon, you and your financial planner will have decided on a route for designing and implementing a financial plan.

PLAN IMPLEMENTATION—THE THIRD INTERVIEW

Either during the mini-marathon or in a conversation over the telephone, decisions have been made about such things as life insurance, investment portfolio, retirement strategies, tax-reduction techniques, and so forth. Each one of these decisions triggers some paperwork to implement the new strategy. This paperwork will probably be handled by one of the financial planner's staff at the office, through the mail, or by the fax machine.

At the third meeting, all the numbers from the initial financial analysis will have been reworked to include the recommended changes. For example, during this third session you will not find a gap between your retirement goals and the strategy to reach those goals (unlike your opening session when you didn't yet have a plan). You and your planner will have created the means to reach those goals.

At this time any contracts or policies or new account statements will be added to your financial organizer, which will become your one source for all your financial information. You will want to bring this organizer with you to each meeting; it not only organizes all the complex information regarding your plan, but it serves as a resource to you and for your family.

For example, one of my long-term clients was a former Baptist minister who lived in the Midwest. When he reached age seventy-five, his health deteriorated. He grew concerned about his family's lack of knowledge regarding his financial plan. During the annual review of his financial plan, he asked, "What do I do about their lack of information?"

I said, "Just give them our phone number. We have copies of everything." When he died, his children called our office, and we brought them up to date on his financial plan. As the financial planning firm for the deceased, we had a complete record of his information. That saved the grieving family countless hours of frustration and anxiety, as well as kept them from having to hire a lawyer to track down all the details of the pastor's financial life.

During this third session, you also review your overall financial plan. Does it still make sense? Are there other adjustments? Are there lingering questions? This interview usually lasts about an hour.

After this third interview, it is simply a matter of monitoring the financial plan.

What's Important About an Annual Review?

It's unfortunate, but life is much too fluid to create a financial plan that lasts "once and for all." There are no rigid thirty-year decisions, and you will be fortunate if you are able to stay most of the course for five years. On the other hand, if you have created a good, well-thought-out plan with competent professional help, then your goals will be sufficiently elastic to easily accommodate the ups and downs of real life.

Life is dynamic—always changing, always moving, always evolving. Dynamic is an excellent concept to apply with your financial plan. That is why your financial goals will also evolve and change.

A financial plan is alive. It grows and matures. It incorporates many different changes along the way. Your goals will change. You might change careers, get married, have children, watch them grow up and leave home, receive an inheritance, take time away from your career, or decide to start your own business. No matter what happens in your life, your financial plan must evolve with you.

Continual changes and innovations in financial products will also require that you have a fresh look at your plan. For example, let's consider a relatively simple instrument like life insurance. Years ago, you could only purchase two types of life insurance—term or whole life. In the late seventies, primarily as a result of the dramatic rise in interest rates, insurance companies unraveled the product. Then they put it back together in very flexible plans. These companies created universal life so the insurance companies could pay a substantially increased rate of interest on the cash value. By 1985, most insurance companies had converted their whole life contract holders to universal life contracts. Then another evolution occurred. As interest rates began to fall and the stock market began to rise, the product was transformed into variable universal life. Through this new product, investors who purchased life insurance contracts could invest their insurance premiums directly into into professionally managed accounts. This innovative, state-of-the-art life insurance contract provides relatively low-cost insurance for the entirety of a person's life but also allows for substantial investment and tax advantages.

Another reason for an annual review—even if there are no life changes or the financial industry hasn't changed—is that more than likely the government has introduced new rules regarding financial matters. Congress is usually not stagnant about financial issues, and laws are constantly changing. The tax laws are continually being revised. During almost two decades that I have been in the financial planning industry, I can recall about ten significant changes regarding Individual Retirement Accounts alone—and that's not counting all the other financial instruments.

A financial plan, like your life plan, is a reflection of you.

CHAPTER 5

How Much Is
Enough Insurance?

The title for this chapter is a perennial question that will be examined in depth through financial planning. In the next few pages I will examine the various types of insurance, and you can use this material to review your own situation. Why should we devote so much attention to the issue of insurance? The apostle Paul wrote Timothy, "If anyone does not provide for his relatives, and especially for his own family, he has denied the faith and is worse than an unbeliever" (1 Timothy 5:8).

Before you can afford to invest a dollar, you must first protect that dollar. Insurance is the wonderful financial instrument that allows us to exchange a potentially profound and unlimited risk for a reasonable cost (i.e., the premium). Because we can transfer this unlimited liability to an insurance company, we are able to live with confidence. We have the assurance that if something tragic happens, then at least we will be financially protected.

Insurance is sometimes maligned as a confusing financial tool. How much do we need? What type should we purchase? How long should we hold a particular type of insurance? What benefits are included in the insurance?

Why Should You Have Insurance?

Before I cover the specifics of insurance, let me issue a warning: One of the main reasons why our country has so many cultural, political, and economic problems today is precisely because the government is doing something that the founding fathers never intended. As individual citizens, we have failed to take responsibility for accumulating sufficient assets to cover our retirement, and we have failed to protect ourselves from the high cost of healthcare with adequate, self-paid insurance protection.

Many people believe they are entitled to healthcare and retirement benefits through government-created programs. Not only is there a cultural cost to shifting responsibility for our financial welfare to the government, but there is also a huge monetary drain. If these entitlement programs were eliminated from the budget of the United States, our country would not only be able to significantly reduce taxes, but it could also run a continual surplus. Fully 49% of the fiscal-1995 budget was earmarked for social welfare programs, and that percentage shows no sign of abating.*

In a free society, each person has an individual responsibility to appropriately manage his own insurance and

---

*US Government Budget, 1995

financial plans. That is not the responsibility of the government. If we fail to take our individual responsibility, then to the extent of that failure, we contribute to the fiscal (and social) decay of our nation. This warning is little discussed in the media, but each of us bears responsibility to consider it.

Regarding insurance, remember two key points. First, be responsible and buy the appropriate insurance that will cover your needs. Second, remember that insurance must be purchased *before you need it.* You have to buy insurance before the risk it is designed to cover actually occurs. You can't wait until you have an auto accident to buy insurance to cover the accident. Nor can you wait until your health deteriorates before you purchase health insurance. If you are ill, no insurance company can reasonably accept you. The lesson is clear: Apply for insurance before you need it and while you are eligible.

For simplicity, I will treat each insurance component separately: (1) liability insurance, (2) homeowner and renter insurance, (3) automobile insurance, (4) disability insurance, (5) long-term care insurance, (6) Medicare supplement insurance, (7) health insurance, and (8) life insurance.

1. LIABILITY INSURANCE

Lawsuits with heavy financial consequences and personal liability are rampant in the United States.

Whether someone trips and falls in your yard, accuses you of slander, gets bitten by your dog, or gets hit by your child, you'd better be prepared to suffer through a lawsuit. All too quickly a simple mishap can turn into a nightmare. Television commercials that feature various attorneys who advertise their legal prowess remind us that each of us is vulnerable to such lawsuits. At present, our best option is to protect ourselves with a personal liability policy. As the book *The ABC's of Managing Your Money* points out, "One of the best ways to protect yourself and your family from personal lawsuits is to purchase a personal liability umbrella insurance policy. The policy usually covers any family member living in your home or away at school and legal defense costs. You will want to consult with your financial advisor about obtaining such a policy." The author, Jonathan Pond, CPA, continues, saying, "A good umbrella policy will protect you, your family members living in your home, children attending school away from home, and even pets. In addition, the policy should cover legal defense costs, critically important since even the successful defense of a lawsuit can be very costly. The best protection against the threat of a lawsuit is to purchase a personal liability umbrella insurance policy."

This liability insurance policy can be purchased at a reasonable cost, depending on the amount of exposure and coverage. This type of policy should give you peace of mind when you watch those video blooper shows that replay a neighbor's car rolling down the sidewalk without a driver—headed toward the swimming pool across the street.

2. Homeowner and Renter Insurance

Your property insurance should cover unexpected loss to your property. Most policyholders tend to be underinsured. Here are some suggested coverage guidelines:

- Homeowner or renter insurance should cover at least 80% of the replacement value of your home, allowing for annual inflation. This coverage will add additional cost to the policy, but it represents a necessary value.

- Your policy should also include replacement-cost coverage for your household contents so that you avoid having to haggle with the insurer over the actual cash value of any losses.

- If you have a special collection such as jewelry, guns, or paintings, you'll want to add a floater policy to your basic contract. This floater policy will cover the value of the collection that exceeds the minimum allowed through the basic plan.

- Be aware that computer equipment and other material used to operate any business inside the home will necessitate additional coverage.

3. AUTOMOBILE INSURANCE

Most automobile insurance policies cover a standard, which meets the minimum needs of most motorists. The following list includes five types of coverage that you will want to make sure are included in your policy:

BODILY INJURY PROPERTY LIABILITY

This insurance covers injury to pedestrians and occupants of other vehicles and damage that you have done to the property of others. Discuss with your insurance agent the proper amount of coverage, being aware that as you accumulate more assets, then you should increase the amount of your insurance.

MEDICAL PAYMENTS INSURANCE

This insurance will cover medical payments on behalf of the policyholder and family members, as well as other passengers in the vehicle. Ask your agent to compare the need for this insurance with what your health insurance policy will cover.

UNINSURED MOTORIST COVERAGE

Although many states require a minimum amount of liability coverage for any vehicle, some motorists disobey this law. Additionally, the minimum required insurance may be less than what is needed to compensate for actual loss. By purchasing this insurance, the policyholder will be covered for both uninsured and underinsured risks from other drivers.

COLLISION INSURANCE

This insurance is usually required on any vehicle with a mortgage or lease. It covers damage to the vehicle regardless of who actually caused the loss. If your vehicle is not financed, you may find it more economical to reduce or eliminate this coverage—particularly if your vehicle has little monetary value.

COMPREHENSIVE INSURANCE

This insurance covers your vehicle from virtually all risks including theft, vandalism, collision with animals, and so forth.

4. DISABILITY INSURANCE

For most working people, the greatest risk probably comes from the loss of income due to a disability. Yet unless the employer provides a good policy, most people do not have nearly sufficient amounts of disability insurance to protect against such a loss.

Disability insurance is designed to replace your lost future wages in the event of an illness, or injury. For example, if you are currently earning $40,000 a year and expect to work for another twenty years, adjusting for inflation at 4%, even without any real increase in your salary, you will earn $1,191,123 during this time period. You and your family will expect at least $1.1 million from your wages over the next twenty years to accomplish your dreams. So if you suddenly became disabled and could not work any longer, your dreams would evaporate. And because you can typically expect an increase in expenses to accompany a disability, those dreams can be transformed into nightmares for the entire family.

Having some amount of disability insurance but not the right kind can also be devastating. I had this fact forever ingrained in my mind with a story I heard shortly after I moved to Nashville. Gary, a thirty-five-year-old husband and father of two, was involved in an accident that paralyzed him from the waist down. Instead of working as a construction foreman, Gary was sitting in a wheelchair. On the one hand, Gary was lucky because he survived the accident. And because he had earlier purchased enough disability insurance, his economic lifestyle did not have to change. On the other hand, however, he wasn't so lucky. His benefit period capped out at five years. Gary was already wrestling with a loss of self-worth. As he faced the termination of his benefits, he grew increasingly distraught. Finally, in the last year of his benefit period, unable to cope with the loss of both his physical abilities and his income, Gary resorted to suicide. He left a note telling his family that he could not bear to watch them suffer the effects of both his physical inability to be a father and husband, and his economic inability to provide for his family.

Disability insurance protects wage earners from adding financial tragedy on top of personal tragedy. Here are some guidelines when shopping for this type of insurance:

- Cover at least 65% of your earnings. If you purchase the policy, any of your benefits from the policy will be tax-free.

- Extend the period of time between when the disability begins and when you can start receiving benefits for as long as your assets will provide for your needs. This coverage will result in reduced premium rates.

- Be sure to add some kind of inflation protection, and update your coverage annually.

- If you are in a specialized field, you may want to add your "own occupation" to the definition of disability. This type of policy will increase your disability insurance expenses, but it will allow you to collect benefits if you cannot perform the primary duties of the job you are working.

5. Long-Term Care Insurance

Like disability insurance, long-term care insurance is designed to protect assets. As the United States population grows increasingly senior, the need will increase for long-term care (LTC) insurance. You cannot depend on Medicare to cover these expenses. Medicare will not cover the costs associated with long-term convalescent care. Unless you intend to pay upward of $40,000 a year for that care from your own assets, you'll need a well-thought-through LTC insurance policy.

Until the late 1980s, insurance companies had scant actuarial information to establish the baselines for benefits and premiums. This situation has changed drastically today. A number of excellent plans are available from reputable and established insurance companies. In fact, today a long-term insurance plan should be purchased through a "building process." There are numerous benefits that can be built into a plan in order to develop just the right package for any insured. For example, some individuals are quite firm that they never want to enter or be treated in a convalescent home. For these individuals, an LTC plan with the primary benefits weighted toward home healthcare will not only allow them to remain in their home while receiving care, but it will also give them an increased peace of mind as they enter their twilight years.

An LTC insurance plan can be customized with many benefits. Because there are too many to address here, I'll instead suggest that you use the following guidelines when considering LTC insurance:

- Be sure you have a sufficient home healthcare provision.
- Extend the coverage for life, not for a period of years.
- Include as few ADL triggers (activities of daily living) benefits as possible.
- Buy LTC insurance early (when you are in your early sixties).

Here is a primary profile of someone who needs this type of insurance. He or she would be approaching retirement with a net worth between $200,000 and $1,000,000. If your net worth is below $200,000, the premiums might be prohibitively expensive when compared to your income. If your net worth is above $1,000,000, it might make more sense to pocket the premium and self-insure. Your individual situation may be different. Seek professional counsel, and involve your children in the decision-making process.

Always remember that you are in the driver's seat. There are almost limitless ways you can arrange benefits to fit your needs. When a salesperson suggests a particular type of LTC policy, don't buy it immediately without some additional research. Contact your state insurance commissioner's office and ask for information about LTC insurance. They will provide you with a pamphlet that details the various features of a LTC policy.

Finally, don't be penny-wise and pound-foolish. What do you need in LTC? Determine this first, and then add benefits that meet your particular goals. For example, let's say you want your insurance to cover your costs for any extended convalescent care. If the average cost for that care in your area is running about $90 per day, don't buy a policy that covers only $65 per day. Additionally, make sure you add an inflation adjustment feature to the policy. In the final analysis, you should shop for what you need, not for what you want to pay in premium.

6. MEDICARE SUPPLEMENT INSURANCE

Medicare supplement insurance is designed to cover the gap between what Medicare will pay in medical-care expenses versus what you'll actually be charged. Because this type of insurance varies from state to state and because it is politically sensitive, it changes frequently. I suggest you contact the state insurance commissioner's office and ask for the information pamphlet on Medicare supplement insurance. It will explain why this coverage is necessary for anyone who is a participant in the Medicare insurance program. Also the pamphlet covers what types of standard policies can be obtained, and how to compare when shopping for this type of insurance.

Be aware of the six-month open-enrollment period surrounding your sixty-fifth birthday. During open enrollment, you will be able to apply for this insurance without having to be approved medically. In other words, you cannot be denied this insurance *if you apply during this period.* If you delay past this six-month window of opportunity you will have to go through an underwriting process, and it is quite possible your application will be turned down due to medical history.

7. HEALTH INSURANCE

Most Americans have health insurance through their employer. Self-employed workers and those workers who are not covered by a group plan will need to buy an individual policy. There are three types of plans on today's market: HMOs (health maintenance organizations), PPOs (preferred provider organizations) and traditional health plans. HMOs and PPOs will be less expensive than a traditional plan, but the policy will not usually be as flexible or as portable as a traditional plan.

The following are some features that you should make sure are part of your health insurance plan:

- Comprehensive coverage that will cover you wherever you need treatment and for whatever ails you. Stay away from the cheaper policies, which cover only certain types of illnesses or injuries.

- Acceptable and definite maximum out-of-pocket cost. Know the amount of your maximum portion for any catastrophic claim.

- Guaranteed renewable. Reputable insurers have a long history in the industry and sell comprehensive policies. Almost always these comprehensive policies include the provision to be guaranteed renewable.

Never buy solely according to the premium! Health insurance is like everything else in a free market—you get what you pay for. Don't shop for the lowest premium until you (a) have the policy provisions that you want, (b) know you are dealing with a financially secure insurer that has been in the healthcare business for many years, and (c) know that you can be approved medically for the policy.

Here's one final thought about health insurance: If you are self-employed, I strongly encourage you to look into a medical savings account (MSA). The government authorized 750,000 of these as an experiment. An MSP has a high deductible ($2,500 to $15,000), which initially sounds like a disadvantage. However, that high deductible is complemented by a tax-deductible contribution to your medical savings account, so that you have the money to make up for the deductible *if* you need it. And here's the great part. If in any year you don't need to use the money you put into the MSA, *you get to keep it!* And keep in mind that it was already a tax-deductible contribution. The bottom line is that you could end up saving thousands of dollars (toward your retirement or other financial goal) that would have otherwise gone to an insurance company to pay the higher premium associated with low-deductible plans. Now *that* is more typical of the American way to address high healthcare costs!

8. LIFE INSURANCE

I've left life insurance until last for a reason. It's the one type of insurance where people have the greatest emotional ties. They say things like, "I don't believe in whole life insurance" or "You should always buy term insurance and invest the difference" (referring to the lesser cost of term insurance versus the higher cost of whole life).

Understand that your life insurance policy has no connection to your belief system. I *believe* in God, but I don't ascribe that same level of value to a simple financial instrument. Life insurance is an exceedingly important instrument in most people's financial plan—that's it and nothing more. Let's examine life insurance on an intellectual level rather than on an emotional level. Unfortunately, if you discuss life insurance with an insurance salesperson, then you'll probably find yourself pulled into an emotional discussion. Have the courage and insight to recognize this pitfall, then direct the discussion to an intellectual level.

Most people are substantially underinsured. They are underinsured for two basic reasons: (1) They don't know how to calculate their true insurance need, and (2) they think that even if they did know their true need, they couldn't afford that amount of insurance. You can solve these two problems easily, but only after getting rid of your biases. Simply determine your need and then shop for the least expensive way to fulfill this need. Here's a good rule of thumb: Your life insurance coverage should be between five and ten times your annual earnings. To meet this need, begin to consider annual renewable term insurance. You will be amazed how inexpensively you can provide the amount of financial security that your family deserves.

There are two additional considerations before you actually purchase the insurance. The first consideration relates to love and the second relates to taxes.

Life insurance might be considered the greatest love letter you could ever write to your family. If the most traumatic event did occur, if a wage-earning spouse/ parent died, the emotional toll on the family would be incalculable. There is no earthly way to mitigate this loss. However, we can substantially eliminate the accompanying financial loss. In fact, I will say that a Christian has a responsibility to make adequate provision for the care of his family even in the event of his death.

Many times I've been discussing the responsibility of life insurance with a couple and I will hear, "Oh, she'd get remarried." Or, "He could get a better job." These kinds of responses project unrealistic optimism in the face of a most tragic event. Instead, I've developed a rule about the decision-making process: Before you decide on how much insurance to purchase, *assume that you are already dead,* sitting with a checkbook in hand, and looking down at your family left on earth. If you could simply, magically write a check and deposit it into your family's account to make sure that the emotional loss was not compounded by economic depravity, what would be the amount of that check? Whatever your answer, that is the amount of insurance you should own.

Life insurance enjoys very special tax treatment. To the extent that your life insurance has a cash value (savings) portion to it such as whole life or universal life, that savings element of the contract will grow tax-deferred. In other words, you will not have to pay income tax on the gain while it accumulates in the policy. In fact, depending on the type of policy and the method used for accessing the cash value, it is possible to never pay any tax on the earnings. Because of the unique tax advantages associated with cash value life insurance, flexible-premium options, and the opportunity to access the cash value virtually on demand, a state-of-the-art cash value insurance policy, such as variable universal life, can be an excellent cornerstone to a developing financial plan.

Let's illustrate the power of the tax-deferral benefit of a variable universal life policy. You determine to save $300 each month for the next twenty years. Investment A is currently taxable, but investment B is tax deferred. In this hypothetical example, we'll assume that both investments receive the same rate of return—say 12% annually. If you are in a 28% tax bracket, at the end of twenty years, investment A would be worth $191,443— but investment B would be worth $296,777. The difference amounts to $105,334. Of course in the case of life insurance we would also have to take into consideration the cost of the insurance. In most cases, however, particularly where the intent is to invest the maximum into the policy that tax law allows, even after considering the yearly cost of the policy, the difference in savings associated with tax deferral makes the variable universal life insurance contract an attractive investment option. If you defer the income tax on your investment gain, it can make a tremendous difference in the ending net value.

Whether to use cash value insurance instead of term or which type of cash value insurance to use and how much to invest are issues well beyond the scope of this chapter. I strongly suggest that you and your financial planner consider this special tax treatment for your life insurance before you determine how to solve your insurance need. Tax-deferred insurance will also be a factor in addressing your long-term savings program.

Here are some general principles that I have used in the area of life insurance planning with my clients. I see whole life insurance as an expensive, inflexible, and obsolete type of insurance. I recommend some form of straight term insurance or universal life insurance, especially if you are considering an investment plan or if you are in a higher tax bracket.

To really give you some insight into what you can do with life insurance as a financial planning tool, I'll give you a peek at what I personally own. I have a variable universal life policy which offers numerous investment options, most of which have distinctively different investment characteristics. These funds represent multiple asset classes, which I have managed by a portfolio management process based on Modern Portfolio Theory. The policy allows me to access the profit from my investment without ever paying any income tax. This is accomplished through a loan provision.

I can access my invested dollars in the policy on a tax-favored basis through borrowing. And because the policy guarantees that I will never be charged more for the loan than I earn in interest on the borrowed funds, I may be able to keep the money and never make any payments—principal or interest—on the loan. Now that's a life insurance policy. You should know that certain situations could occur to cause the loss of these tax benefits—again underscoring the importance of relying on professional financial planning assistance.

Several years ago I was involved in one of the most interesting applications of this concept. One day a young, single doctor in his mid-thirties came into my office for some financial assistance. By most people's standards, this doctor was well-to-do. His investment portfolio approached $1 million, but his income taxes were so high that he felt as if he were spinning his wheels. By the time his loss of personal exemptions and deductions were accounted for, and then both the highest state and federal income tax rate were applied, he was only able to keep about 55 cents of every dollar he made (whether from his investments or wages). I proposed that this doctor fund a variable universal life policy. The tax laws calculate the maximum contribution allowable to a VUL in any year without reducing or eliminating the income tax advantages. In his case, we set up the VUL so that he contributed $90,000 a year. With that amount going in, the death benefit of the policy turned out to be $2,791,574.

Obviously this young, single professional with a million-dollar investment portfolio didn't need that much life insurance. In fact, you could argue that he didn't need any life insurance at all. But he did need income tax help, and the VUL policy gave him such assistance. He did well on the earnings over the next five years, averaging about 12%. And he didn't have to pay a dime in taxes.

At the end of the fifth year, he had accumulated over $472,000 in his cash value. If you subtract out the $364,000 in premiums he paid in this period, he still gained about $108,000. Now if the same dollars that were invested in the variable universal life policy had been invested instead in, say, a taxable investment averaging the same 12%, the gain would have only been $55,119. And keep in mind not only did the young doctor gain an extra $52,000 over the taxable equivalent, but he also had the benefit of a $2.7 million insurance benefit!

This example is for illustration purposes only. To determine whether a variable universal life policy is in your best interest, you and your financial advisor should carefully review the pros and cons of such a policy.

Here's the bottom line regarding insurance: Commit to purchasing enough life insurance so that if you die prematurely your family will be financially secure. Don't be afraid of the premiums. If you buy the policy when you are healthy, term insurance is very inexpensive. If you choose the more expensive method of providing life insurance benefits through a cash value product such as variable universal life, recognize that there are many creative ways of paying for it that can have a very positive impact on your overall financial plan.

Before I leave the section on life insurance, I want to address one more issue, and that is the question of whether children should have life insurance. I'll give you my answer with a story of an incident that happened a few years ago. Early in my career, my employer developed a program that allowed its insureds to convert their whole life policy for the more state-of-the-art universal life policy. In most cases, this was definitely in their best interest. I was contacting all the insureds in my territory about the program.

One of these families had two parents and three little girls. They lived on a farm in rural eastern Colorado, and were, by community standards, of moderate income. I also knew them as members of our church. They considered the program and decided it was something they wanted to do. In the process, I provided each of them with increases in coverage, including the girls. In fact, the small $5,000 policies for the children were converted to $25,000 policies. I remember thinking that amount would be something they could take with them into their new families in the years to come.

One Sunday about four months later as the prayers were being said, the pastor began praying for one of the little girls who had just been diagnosed with leukemia. Startled, I made a mental note to check on the policy to make sure it was issued and in order. Thankfully, everything was in order. The little girl's condition deteriorated, and the prognosis was not good. The parents made continuous visits to Denver for the little girl's chemotherapy. Each trip took all day, since drive time alone was five hours, plus the hours at the hospital for treatment and recovery. Eventually, two days turned into four days. The situation got so bad that people in the community and church began helping do the farm chores, including the arduous irrigating by hand that had to be done in that dry climate.

One day I stopped by their house to check on them. When I knocked on the white-frame farmhouse door, the mother greeted me and asked me to come inside. As the three little girls played outside on the trampoline, she began to give me an update, and her eyes filled with tears. Suddenly, we heard a scream and ran to the door only to see the sick five-year-old girl jumping on the trampoline crying at the top of her lungs, "I'm going to die, I'm going to die, I'm going to die."

The two sisters just watched, and the mother bolted out the door to wrap the poor girl in her comforting arms.

As I silently walked to my car, I saw all four of them in one big family hug, crying and holding on to each other.

About six months later, the little girl died. Again, I made my way out to that white farmhouse and knocked on the door. The mother and father both came to greet me, but no words were spoken. They knew why I was there. I handed them the check for $25,000 and whispered, "I'm so, so sorry."

The mother with tears streaming down her face hugged me and I departed. Later I found out that because the cancer treatment was considered experimental, their health insurance did not cover over $100,000 of their bills. And with the enormous costs of running a farm as an absentee owner, the family was in debt well beyond anything that $25,000 could begin to cover.

Do I believe children should have insurance? You bet! How much insurance? Enough coverage to pay for their funeral and to cover any expenses associated with the parents focusing away from their occupation and on the physical health of their sick child. The insurance should also cover the emotional health of the family—for a long time to come. Don't skimp on this important area of life insurance. The potential cost of bypassing this coverage is simply much higher than you can imagine.

CHAPTER 6

Choose the Right
Investment Strategy

Several years ago, a highly successful NCAA coach was referred to me. Jack, along with his wife, Anne, had made a fairly good income over the years and was approaching retirement. Anne was an accountant, and considerably younger than he. His investment program consisted of an employer-provided retirement benefit, an employer provided defined-contribution plan similar to a 401(k), mutual funds, and individual stocks. He asked me to review his program and make recommendations.

After meeting with him and his wife, I made the following suggestions:

- Purchase a variable universal life insurance policy. This will allow Jack to take the maximum income from his defined-benefit plan at retirement without having to reduce it in order to provide income for Anne in the event he predeceased her (which would be likely). Instead, and if he did predecease her, the life insurance benefit would pick up where the defined benefit left off. In the event that she predeceased him, he would have the option of canceling the insurance and getting the cash value returned to him, or changing the beneficiary to someone else (such as children).

- Reduce the amount that was in the money market mutual fund from $40,000 to $10,000, and move the $30,000 to a managed mutual fund portfolio.

- Move a considerable amount to a combination of investments that are not subject to market risk, such as triple-net-lease real estate programs, tax credit programs, and an oil and gas program. These would not only further diversify his portfolio, but also give him cash flow, and substantial income tax relief— both now and in the future.

- Convert much of the remaining mutual funds and stock portfolio to variable annuities coupled with professional asset allocation. This would reduce his income tax liability on a current basis and for all future years, since now he would only be taxed on what he actually *spent,* not on what he earned.

With an eye toward retirement, we developed an investment program that reduced his overall risk through diversification, increased his pension income through providing survivor benefits from insurance, substantially reduced his income tax liability for many years to come, and increased his opportunity to achieve a higher return on his portfolio. Jack and Ann were pleased and felt more confident about the future.

The topic of investments is filled with endless categories of opportunities such as stocks, bonds, mutual funds, Individual Retirement Accounts (IRAs), 401(k)s, tax sheltered annuities, limited partnerships, oil and gas programs, tax credits, gold and precious metals. Add to all the investment options their various income tax consequences, and on top of that all the different types of risk, and it is easy to see why people become quickly frustrated. It's difficult to know where to begin, how to tell if you're making the right decisions, and whether you're taking too much risk.

Each of the investments listed in the last paragraph is neither right nor wrong. Rather, each investment is only appropriate or inappropriate. For example, an investment in a natural gas program, which is considered speculative, for someone who has no liquidity and little net worth, would be inappropriate. However, that same natural gas program might be a quite appropriate investment when used as a part of a strategy to reduce taxable income for an investor with ample liquidity, a strong net worth, and suffering from the effects of a sale of taxable, appreciated stock. Each investment has its own unique characteristics, advantages, and disadvantages. Whether a particular investment should be included in your financial plan should be dictated more by the objectives of your individual situation than by the characteristics of a particular investment. Developing an appropriate investment plan requires a systematic and logical process. Christians, who too often tend to invest emotionally rather than logically, need to remember this principle of appropriateness.

An investor should not purchase a certificate of deposit (CD) simply because it is FDIC (Federal Deposit Insurance Corporation) insured. Similarly, an investor should not refrain from investing in mutual funds simply because their value fluctuates. Rather, the question of whether to invest in either a CD or mutual funds, as well as the questions of when and in what amounts and for what duration, should be approached solely on the basis of the objectives of your plan. How much money do you need? When do you need it? Will you need it in a lump sum or over a period of time? Should the needs of anyone else be considered? How will this investment be funded—as a single deposit or in monthly installments? What are the income tax considerations?

Consider the process of how you decide to dress yourself each day. Do you say to yourself, "I like flannel shirts. I'm going to wear a flannel shirt today"? Or do you consider first the weather, and then look at the various options you have for that particular climactic condition? Obviously, if you live in Dallas, it's August, and you decide to wear that flannel shirt, you're going to roast! And so it is with the process of determining how to structure your investment program. Before you say "I like CDs," you should look at the financial climate you'll be wearing that CD in before you commit to it. What if CDs are only paying 4%, you are in a high tax bracket, and you are investing long term? That scenario is just as ridiculous from an investment perspective as if you were in Dallas in the summer and walked outside with a heavy, long-sleeved flannel shirt!

Do You Have a Financial Junk Drawer?

The investment portfolio of many people looks like a junk drawer. At home, your junk drawer probably includes various unorganized items, a ruler, a flashlight, a tape measure, a rubber band, a pencil. You never know what you will find when you open it, because there is little sense of commonality among the items. Similarly, your investment portfolio might include a savings account, an IRA, a mutual fund, some stock, an annuity. You purchased each item somewhere along your journey of life for reasons that seemed perfectly logical at the point of purchase. Maybe a friend went into the insurance business or your father recommended a mutual fund or your boss suggested a certain stock. Now as you consider your overall investment strategy, you begin to wonder if your program makes sense. You are asking a good question.

Investing on Purpose

"The best way to predict the future is to create it." There is only one reason to invest, and that is to provide financial resources to fund your life goals. Although this may sound self-evident, most people fail to check their investment decisions against this touchstone. Instead, they fall into the trap of looking for the "best" investments—without regard to whether they are appropriate to their individual plan.

Let's consider an example of how life goals appropriately dictate investment decisions. For our example, consider the ubiquitous retirement-planning scenario that most Americans wrestle with. Please keep in mind that the actual numbers I'll present are hypothetical. Each individual investor needs to consider various risk factors before deciding to invest in any program. There is no assurance you would actually achieve similar results. Additionally, in the interest of simplifying the examples, income taxes have not been factored into the formulas.

We'll say your retirement objective is $4,000 a month beginning in twenty years and that this amount will need to continue for the balance of your life—say thirty years after that. Your first task will be to consider inflation. The $4,000 a month in 1999 is something quite different from an equal amount of purchasing power in twenty years. In fact, after adjusting for an inflation rate of 4%, you will need $8,765 the first month of your retirement if you want the same purchasing power as $4,000 today! And, because of inflation, that $8,765 will continuously go up.

When I present this scenario before a live audience, I usually encounter some degree of disbelief regarding the numbers. So don't take my word for it, just take a look back in time to 1954. In that year, a U.S. first-class postage stamp cost 3 cents, the average family car could be purchased for just over $2,700, and a loaf of bread cost 17 cents. The difference between the prices in 1954 and the cost of these same items today is the effect of inflation.

The second task involves adding up all the potential income sources that will be available to help make up your retirement income. These sources might include a company sponsored retirement plan such as a 401(k), or an individual program such as an IRA. There may also be a pension or annuity benefit. You may or may not want to include Social Security benefits. I am of the opinion that the Social Security system as it exists today in 1999 will be dramatically altered within a few years. Based on current funding and benefit projections, it will literally be impossible for Social Security to pay benefits to me that have been promised (I was born in 1955). Therefore, if you were born in 1950 or later, you might want to eliminate consideration of Social Security benefits from your available retirement income sources.

After you have all these projected values, you can then subtract this amount from your desired retirement-income ($8,890 per month).

Your third and final task involves accounting for the difference between your desired retirement income and your available retirement income. For example, let's assume your available retirement income will be $5,700 a month. Since your desired monthly income is $8,890, you will need to find a solution for the difference, which is $3,190 per month.

Now we have reached the interesting part of this process. How much money must you accumulate in the next twenty years in order to produce $3,190 a month for the rest of your life? (To simplify this example, we are not adjusting for inflation.) We'll assume a thirty-year post-retirement life (in other words, the moment you use all your money will be the moment you leave this earth). *The answer to this question will be entirely contingent on the rate of return your retirement savings will be earning.* If you are able to achieve a 6% rate of return, you will need to have $534,726 on deposit the day you retire. However, if you are able to achieve an 8% return, you would only need $437,643. And a rate of return of 12% would require that you have $313,228 on deposit on the day you retire. You can see what a tremendous difference the rate of return makes on your overall financial position. And that impact is even more noticeable if we carry this scenario to the present and consider how much you will need to invest each month between now and your retirement in order to reach your goal.

Once again, the means to answering this question relates to the rate of return on your investment. A goal of $534,726 in twenty years will require a monthly investment of $1,157 at a 6% rate of return. If you are able to achieve an 8% return on your investment and have a goal of $437,643, your monthly investment will need to be $743. And at 12% with a goal of $313,228, you will only need to invest a manageable $317.

Figure 6-1

How much will you need to invest each month at different rates of return for the next 20 years to reach your accumulation goal that will provide $3,190 per month?* *

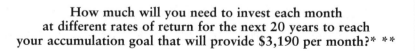
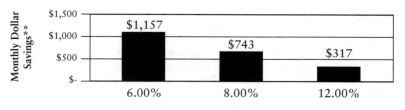

* These figures do not reflect the cost of insurance, monthly contract charge and premium tax charges, which vary with each individual policy; if they did, the performance quoted would be significantly lower. Please note the above illustration is hypothetical, and is not intended to be a projection of future value.

** Taxes, fees, expenses and market volatility are not reflected.

Figure 6-2

How much money must you accumulate in 20 years to produce $3,190 a month for 30 years at different rates of return?* **

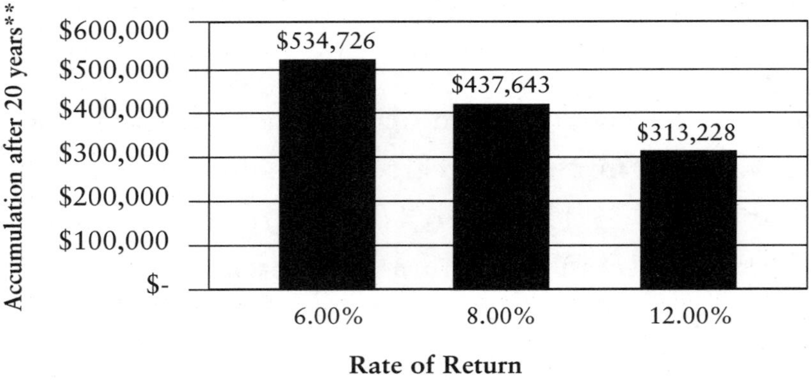

* These figures do not reflect the cost of insurance, monthly contract charge and premium tax charges, which vary with each individual policy; if they did, the performance quoted would be significantly lower. Please note the above illustration is hypothetical, and is not intended to be a projection of future value.

** Taxes, fees, expenses and market volatility are not reflected.

Bottom line is that you should always try to earn as high a return as you can with your long-term investing, while at the same time not take any unnecessary risk. Everyone needs a planned strategy for his investments. Otherwise, the strategy that you will end up with will have only coincidental relevance to your life plan. I am reminded of the political adage, "If you don't stand for something, you'll fall for anything." Similarly, if you don't hold to an investment plan, you'll end up being courted by every type of investment philosophy that crosses your path. That can be very dangerous, and it is certainly at odds with *Money for Life.*

CHAPTER 7

Select the Right
Investments

George and Nancy came to my office to talk about their financial plan. They were unsure about the effectiveness of their plan and were looking for a second opinion. One of their investments was in a low-income housing (IRS Code Sec. 42) tax credit program. As a general rule, I like tax credit programs, assuming they meet due diligence requirements and are appropriate for the financial plan of the investor. The problem here was that these two people had invested almost 40% of their cash assets in the program and, worse, had bought the program on an installment plan. This meant that they would pay a high interest rate over ten years on monthly installments just to get some tax credits. And to add insult to injury, they were cash strapped, couldn't use all the credits the program was generating, and couldn't liquidate the investment! The only way they could ever make this scenario work was to increase their income—substantially.

In this chapter I will present a number of popular investment vehicles. Consider this information introductory and not comprehensive. My intent is to get you started toward the process of making appropriate investment choices. Before you actually invest, always read the product information carefully and seek professional counsel. I have arbitrarily created five categories of investment options that exist today: (1) stocks and bonds, (2) mutual funds, (3) variable insurance products, (4) limited partnerships, and (5) bank instruments.

1. STOCKS AND BONDS

Buying stock is, quite literally, buying a piece (a share) of a corporation. Average Americans began investing frequently in the stock market after World War II. Owning a stock portfolio of blue-chip companies like General Electric or Ford Motor Company provided many American households investment returns to help supplement their retirement income. Today, the percentage of Americans owning stock is greater than at any other time in our history.

If you asked a grandparent how they bought their stocks over the years, they would most likely say, "Through my broker." Although stockbrokers continue to buy-sell-trade in stocks, an increasing number of investors are trading stock on their own, particularly on the Internet. This is not necessarily a good thing. Although the investor might save substantially on commissions, they also forfeit experience and research in the process.

A form of stock purchase that is becoming more popular, and which probably would not have been included in your grandparents' portfolio, is the initial public offering (IPO). This is one of the riskiest stock purchases you can make, although it could also be the most lucrative. There is so much money in our economy today that there is historic opportunity for start-up companies to find capital in the market. Technology is creating new methods of developing and meeting consumer demand. Societal and cultural change is dramatic. All this adds up to new companies producing new goods and services and getting funding by selling part of their company through stock.

I believe that virtually every investment strategy should contain some amount of stock. How much, from what companies, and in what "package" (outright, through a mutual fund, or in a wrap account) is something only you and your advisor will be able to know.

Bonds are the flip side of stock. Buying a bond from a company is the same as loaning that company your money. Normally, you'll receive interest (coupon) on the bond, and you may be able to sell it before it matures. If after you purchase the bond, interest rates go down and you decide to sell your bond, you'll probably make a profit. Conversely, if you decide to sell after interest rates rise, you'll probably not get what you paid for it.

I am not a big fan of buying bonds if you do not plan to hold them until maturity. Bonds, when cashed in before maturity, can become more or less risky. Corporate bonds can become more or less risky during the time you own them, and you may or may not benefit from that. You may not even know about it. And even if the bond's rating doesn't change, the interest-rate environment certainly will, which means that regardless of whether or not you choose to sell during that period, there will be opportunity risk (explained later). Government bonds are safer, but they also pay little interest. That means that if inflation increases, the value of your interest on the bond is reduced. Statistics illustrate that over the course of a decade or more, stocks are a better buy than bonds. Of course, there are always exceptions.

2. MUTUAL FUNDS

By far the most popular investment today for the average American household are mutual funds. From their beginning in 1924, they offered the same advantages as stocks and bonds. The best way to think of mutual funds is as a professionally managed portfolio of stocks and bonds. When you invest in a mutual fund, you hand over your money to the manager of the fund, who then looks over the financial landscape and buys, sells, and trades your money in the stock and bond markets for you. You benefit from professional management, diversification, and liquidity, since you can sell (redeem) your shares at will. For all these benefits, the Mutual Fund may charge sales load, management fees, and operating expenses. A good manager could possibly outperform anything you might be able to do on your own.

Mutual funds are very popular and there are thousands from which you can select. Each fund will specialize, or focus, on one particular element of economic opportunity. For example, some will invest mostly in companies of a certain size (small capitalization, large capitalization), a certain geography (Far East, Europe, Latin America), specific industry (technology, Internet, health services), and so on. In order to have a proper mutual fund portfolio I recommend that you invest in several different categories of funds. Optimally, those categories should be determined by the science of Modern Portfolio Theory.

The most important development in mutual fund investing in recent years is the advent of values-based investing. I'll have much to say about this in a later chapter. Technology now allows investors the opportunity to consider not only what investment return they want to attempt to achieve, but also what values they want to support with their money. For example, if you suffered through the death of a family member who died of cancer after years of smoking, you might not want your money to be invested in tobacco companies. Similarly, if you support the efforts of your local crisis pregnancy center, you might not want your money invested in companies that manufacture abortifacients or are financial contributors to Planned Parenthood. Keep in mind that the vast majority of mutual fund managers are not going to consider personal values in their investment process, so you'll need to access technology that will allow you to compare mutual funds' investments with your values. The Internet site <http://www.moneyandvalues.com> was developed specifically with that capability for comparison in mind.

Mutual funds can be purchased outright or through a number of "wrappers" such as IRAs, 401(k) plans, and insurance products.

3. VARIABLE INSURANCE PRODUCTS

The popularity of mutual funds in the 1970s gave birth to a revolution in the insurance industry. Annuities and cash value life insurance, long recognized as poor investment options, gained a new life by using professionally managed accounts to determine investment performance. The consequence of this was nothing short of historic. In fewer than fifteen years, variable annuities have grown to over 868 billion in assets. And whereas there were only a handful of insurance companies offering variable products ten years ago, today there are hundreds. (Tillinghast-Towers Perrin, 1st Quarter Report 2001)

Variable Annuities provide many of the benefits of fixed annuities, including tax deferred earnings and a choice of payouts. In addition, they offer the potential for greater returns and the opportunity to make your own decisions on how to allocate your assets among investment portfolios. In their most basic form these investment portfolios are Mutual Funds, either designed specifically for the annuity company or similar versions of existing funds designated for retirement accounts. The primary benefit of this marriage is that the investor does not incur income tax on any gain in the mutual funds until he takes that gain out. So the investor benefits from a compounding return on a tax-deferred basis. This advantage can be substantial. For example, if you were in a 28% tax bracket and you invested $20,000 into an investment that earned 12% over twenty years and were taxed on the earnings each year, your investment would be worth $104,911. By comparison, if you invested the same amount over the same period of time in a variable annuity that had the same return, because you were not taxed along the way your investment would be worth a whopping $192,926. To be fair, there would be mortality expenses on the variable annuity that you might not have on the other investment. So, if we rerun the equation and reduce the 12% return by 1.4% (which might reflect those expenses), you still end up with $150,014. These figures are not based on historical market data and are strictly hypothetical. Always consult the prospectus for specific fund history prior to making any investments decisions. These figures do not reflect the specific tax differences between Mutual Funds and Variable Annuities. Even though Variable Annuities can be tax-deferred. Taxes still may be due at the time of withdrawal. Always consult with your financial advisor and review the prospectus for specific tax ramifications before making any investment decisions.

Variable Annuities also have the benefit of insurance in case you die while the stock market is down. Each company's insurance is different, but the idea is that your heirs are protected somewhat in the event the market value of the annuity's Mutual Funds is below what was originally invested. Some of the disadvantages of Variable Annuities include surrender charges in the first six to ten years if you decide you want to cash out early, and a 10% tax penalty if you pull money out prior to age fifty-nine and a half.

Variable Universal life is similar to Variable Annuities in that you replace a poorly performing insurance company account with mutual funds to determine investment return. Variable Universal Life also offers one tax advantage that no other financial instrument offers, and that is the potential to receive most of your investment gain entirely tax free. Succinctly put, you can borrow the earnings from the value of your mutual funds in your variable life contract, and since that is technically a loan, it is not considered taxable income by the IRS. This makes it possible to continue to borrow throughout your retirement to supplement your income, and then have the death benefit pay the loan off at your death. Since death proceeds from life insurance policies are generally received free from income tax, you would have paid no tax on the mutual fund earnings during your lifetime, and there would be no tax on the death proceeds, either. There are actually some contracts that also offer very low or even no interest on the money you borrow from your contract.

Of course, the above illustration involves a high degree of professional competency. If you are not a financial services professional, you should consult someone with specific competency in this area. There are numerous pitfalls that you would need to avoid when considering such a program.

4. LIMITED PARTNERSHIPS

In the early 1980s, limited partnerships were used primarily as tax shelters and only incidentally as economic investments. That all changed with tax reform laws in 1987. In fact, most limited partnerships created prior to the Tax Reform Act of 1986 imploded as a result, causing enormous financial repercussions. Today, limited partnerships primarily offer economic return and only incidental tax advantages.

Because of their volatile past, limited partnerships have taken a beating in the media. In actuality, limited partnerships offer many investment opportunities in real estate, oil and gas exploration, and leasing operations. Whether any limited partnership opportunity is right for you should be determined only after careful examination. These instruments usually have less liquidity than other investment programs, and there is no secondary market such as the New York Stock Exchange to sell it on if you decide you want out.

5. Bank Instruments

The banking industry's share of the investment market has, appropriately, been reduced in recent years. Banks offer savings accounts, certificates of deposit, and money market funds as typical investment choices. These instruments should not be considered when designing a long-term (five or more years) investment program. Rather, these instruments should be used for short-term needs.

It is unfortunate that so many elderly people still consider the value of FDIC insurance an overriding benefit. It ends up costing them so much that their lifestyle suffers as a result. They forget that the price they pay for that insurance is "opportunity cost," that is, the amount they could have earned with a different investment. Let's look at this a bit more carefully, because I fear that too many older Christians are suffering through a less-than-enjoyable retirement for lack of this knowledge.

Jack Grimes wanted guaranteed security. He did not want to be concerned about the market, so at age fifty-five and approaching retirement, Jack moved all his savings ($200,000) into CDs. At age sixty-two, Jack decided to retire and enjoy his remaining years by spending time with his grandchildren. In those seven years prior to retirement, Jack's CDs averaged 5% return and had grown to $281,420. Jack decided he didn't want to touch the principal and would live off of the interest. Beginning the first month of his retirement, Jack received a monthly check from his bank in the amount of $833.33 ($200,000 x 5% /

12 months = $833.33). Five years into his retirement, Jack began having to cut back on things because inflation was causing prices to go up—but his income remained the same. By age seventy, Jack could barely make ends meet. And ten years after retirement, Jack could no longer afford to travel by air to see his grandchildren—the price of air travel had become too expensive. All his life Jack had looked forward to enjoying his retirement. Now he knew he could very well reach poverty well before he ran out of time.

If Jack had invested his $200,000 in mutual funds, or variable annuities that returned an average of 12% (admittedly with no guarantees) instead of opting for the low return on an FDIC guaranteed bank instrument, by the time Jack retired, his account would have been worth $442,136! The earnings on that account at 12% would have provided Jack a monthly retirement check of $4,421 instead of $833! And because his money was invested in the form of mutual funds, chances are that the underlying value of the funds would have kept pace with inflation.

So next time you hear someone tout the benefit of having money invested in a CD that is backed up by FDIC insurance, remember what that guarantee really costs.

Some Answers to Your Secret Wish

Because I've worked in the financial planning industry for almost two decades, I know what you're wanting at this point. Despite all my rhetoric about choosing investments as they apply to your specific life goals and not on their individual characteristics, you still have a desire to know what blanket suggestions I might have. You're probably secretly wishing for some kind of benchmark, such as what percent should be invested in what types of investments. Unfortunately, prudent financial planning and investment selection is a highly complex process. Nothing I would suggest should be taken to apply to everyone. I stress that each situation is different. However, here are a few general comments that will help guide you in that process:

- Defer income taxes where possible. Use tax-deferred investments such as variable annuities instead of investments that are currently taxable.
- Be careful not to allocate more than a maximum of 20% of your portfolio to limited partnerships.
- Similarly, use 10% of your portfolio as a benchmark for speculative ventures such as IPOs.
- Consider a Variable Universal Life policy as a fundamental building block in your financial plan. Supplement that with as much term insurance as you need, and put as much cash into the contract's subaccounts as tax laws allow.

Use mutual funds as your primary investment strategy. Find a professional who can help you allocate your investment in mutual funds using asset allocation technology. It's a solid, proven fundamental strategy that you can use to move ahead with *Money for Life.*

CHAPTER 8

Investment
Risk

One day, John Scout attended one of my seminars on prudent financial principles. I concentrated on Modern Portfolio Theory (MPT), which, fundamentally, contends that you should not put all your investments in one place. Toward the end of these seminars, I always have an open question-and-answer session.

In his mid-fifties, John stands about six-foot-one and weighs 250 pounds. He stood and leaned on his hands, which were clenched in fists, and said, "I want you to answer one question. What kind of a retirement will you guarantee me in one year, three years, and five years if I turn over all my money to you—and I've got about $700,000."

His question was a minefield. First, I can't guarantee anybody anything. It's against the law even if I thought I could do it. Second, I don't ever discuss an individual situation in a public forum. And third, I didn't know anything more about John so I couldn't know exactly what I would do with his investment portfolio. I invited him to come to my office, and he did.

I met John late in 1993 and we spent several hours in different appointments discussing investment theory. All John's money was locked in certificates of deposits (CDs) or bank instruments. He was appalled at his low rate of return for his investments—yet at the same time he was frightened of the stock market. He made a significant amount of money each year ($150,000), and was looking forward to retiring in the next three years.

John was caught between wanting to protect and not risk his money on the one hand, and yet on the other hand needing to improve his investment return so that he could afford his lifestyle when he retired. I spent most of my time explaining the principles of the market. My goal was for John to be comfortable with the move from bank instruments into stocks, bonds, mutual funds, and market-based investments.

John finally agreed a movement into the market was his wisest course of action. In late 1993, we devised an investment portfolio, which invested about 70% of his money into market-based instruments.

Immediately there was a problem: In 1994, the market tanked. Under the leadership of Alan Greenspan, the Federal Reserve did something completely new—it raised interest rates that year a total of five times. Each time, the raise had a significant adverse affect on the market. In the middle of these changes, John Scout was not happy.

From time to time, John stormed into my office, abruptly confronted my staff, then demanded an appointment with me. Each time, I simply repeated the principles of Modern Portfolio Theory—and urged John to hold the course. I'm glad to report that John lasted (as did I!) through this up-and-down period of the stock market. The markets not only recovered but also rebounded with good profits over the succeeding several years, and John became one of my best clients.

When it comes to investing, there was no amount of information that I could give John Scout in advance to prepare him for this transformation. There is an emotional side and an intellectual side to investing, and as much as possible, we want to eliminate the emotional side. The emotional side is where you get your reason to invest in the first place—you want to retire at a certain point or you want a certain lifestyle or you want a second home. These reasons are an appropriate use of emotion for *motivating* our investing—but they should not affect the investment decision or management process.

When you begin to actually make your investments and manage them, you need to switch into the intellectual process. Intellectually, the volumes of information that exist regarding investment and portfolio management unanimously state that when markets go down, they will also come back up. From time to time, investing has short-term losses (sometimes significant short-term losses), but if you hang on to the investment, more times than not you will be much better off. In fact, it's prudent to invest when the markets go down, because the price you pay will be a bargain. Then when they rebound, you will have even more profit potential. This stock market fluctuation is based on historical data, known as the four stages of the business cycle. [*Dearborn License Exam Manual, Series 6 - 19th Edition*, p. 87].

How do you know when the markets are going to completely bottom out and when it's time to withdraw your funds? You don't.

Back in the 1970s, one of my track coaches at the University of Alabama was taken with the notion that we were nearing the end of the world. He was enamored with Hal Lindsey, a best-selling author who claimed to know the date of the apocalyptic end of the earth. Hal Lindsey believed that current world events were happening in the way that the Bible predicted would foretell the end of time. Yet if you objectively read the Bible about the end times, you will find this: "Now, brothers, about times and dates we do not need to write to you, for you know very well that the day of the Lord will come like a thief in the night" (1 Thessalonians 5:1–2).

No one knows the date of the end of the world, not even Jesus Christ, the Son of God. So, I thought, how can some best-selling author know? This same discussion about the end times is an excellent metaphor for investing. Some doomsayers are heralding that the market is going to crash. Other people are predicting that the stock market will go through 20,000 during the next five years. I recommend that you don't follow either extreme. Instead, I recommend that you follow a prudent course of investing and recognize that:

- No one has ever been able to consistently time the direction of the market.
- No one has ever been able to determine the size of the directional movement.

Timing and direction cannot be determined in advance. The market will go up and it will go down. I recommend that you invest prudently and invest for the long haul.

At another seminar in late 1994, I met a couple in their late fifties, Don and Nita Burns, who were nearing retirement age. They had approximately $600,000—$300,000 of it was in bank instruments (CDs) and the other $300,000 was coming in a lump sum distribution as an early retirement offer from Don's employer.

Because they didn't have much experience with investing, they were concerned about their retirement income. This retirement came early and was not anticipated. Don's health was failing because of late-onset diabetes, and they wanted to enjoy whatever years ahead in retirement.

I calculated their income using only fixed instruments such as fixed annuities and CDs versus investing half of their funds in fixed instruments and half in market-based instruments such as mutual funds.

The Burnses liked the potential return from a market-based investment portfolio, but they were apprehensive about the risk element in the market. As with John Scout, I spent a significant amount of time with them in education about the history of the stock market and how an investor can reduce his overall risk by utilizing Modern Portfolio Theory.

They decided to take "the plunge" (their term) and go with a market-based investment portfolio. The Burnses took this direction in the hopes of being able to live more comfortably in their retirement.

During late 1994 the market was booming, so the Burnses were quickly pleased with the returns on their market-based portion of the investment portfolio. Over the succeeding months, the Burns increased their confidence about the stock market. In fact, their confidence grew to the point that Don and Nita began to regret not having allocated 100% of their retirement portfolio into an asset-allocation investment program. Over the next three years, the Burnses gradually moved everything to the asset allocation portfolio. They have been very pleased with the results of taking this managed-risk approach.

When the Burns began this process, I later learned that Don's first thought every morning was to call the toll-free number of the investment company and check on the daily value of his portfolio. Early on, any day that he found that he had lost money, Nita reported that Don was upset about it. As evidence of his increased confidence in the investment plan, two years later, Don was not making those daily phone calls.

Explore Investment Risk

While we can't plan for the unexpected, we can maintain a realistic view of investment risk. Concern about risk can paralyze Christians. They fear making a mistake—which is really ironic. Solomon, the wisest man on the earth, contended that time and chance happen to everyone. "I have seen something else under the sun: The race is not to the swift or the battle to the strong, nor does food come to the wise or wealth to the brilliant or favor to the learned; but time and chance happen to them all" (Ecclesiastes 9:11).

Life is full of chance and risk. It seems better to eliminate as much risk as possible in an effort to try to reduce anxiety. Larry Wilson points out in his corporate seminars, "You can choose to live your life in an effort to not lose, or you can live your life to win."

Much of the decision process about risk will ultimately affect the difference between living a purposeful life or merely existing. Risk, whether in life, or investing, is inevitable. Approach it with care, prudence, and awareness, but don't allow the fear of it to control you.

As you consider various investments, different types of risk will confront you. Each risk needs to be investigated. *Market risk* is what you accept when you invest in a variable investment that fluctuates in value, like a stock or mutual fund. *Purchasing-power risk* is what you assume when you invest all your resources in something that holds little prospect for growth, like a savings account or money-market fund. *Opportunity risk* is the difference between what you could have earned in a different, higher risk, higher-producing investment versus the lower risk, lower producing investment you actually made. *Financial risk* and *business risk* are specific and singular investments in one company or one industry. This risk can be eliminated almost entirely through diversification. Finally, *liquidity risk* is an investment that is not easily redeemable on demand.

Each investment holds some form of risk. It is impossible to eliminate all risk. However, it is both possible and prudent to manage your risk through a properly developed and well-managed investment program. Don't let your concern for risk paralyze you. It is possible to make some mistakes along the way and still come out better than if you chose what appeared to be the safe alternative. Remember the story about Peter and Thomas in Chapter 2?

Income Taxes and Investing

One day the Pharisees set out to trap Jesus with a question. They asked, "Tell us then, what is your opinion? Is it right to pay taxes to Caesar or not?" (Matthew 22:17). Jesus took a minute and asked them to show him the coin and tell him whose picture was on the coin.

"Caesar's," they replied.

Then Jesus astounded them with his answer saying, "Give to Caesar what is Caesar's, and to God what is God's" (Matthew 22:21). The United States Tax Code places the burden of determining how much is "Caesar's" on each individual citizen. I am distressed to hear naive Christians with good intentions proclaim they gladly pay their taxes. Sometimes this kind of attitude camouflages the fact that too much tax is being paid unnecessarily.

How much tax is enough is a philosophical issue. It came before the courts in 1947 in Commissioner versus Newman when Justice Learned Hand wrote, "Over and over again courts have said that there is nothing sinister in so arranging one's affairs as to keep taxes as low as possible. Everyone does so, rich or poor, and all do right, for nobody owes any public duty to pay more than the law demands: Taxes are enforced extractions, not voluntary contributions. To demand more in the name of morals is mere cant." So from both the words of Jesus and the tax court, we can proceed to review the U.S. income tax system and hold the philosophical premise that while we should pay our taxes, we should not pay any more tax than required.

There are few absolutes in the world of investment planning. There is one axiom, however, that comes pretty close to an absolute: Never make an investment exclusively on the basis of tax implications. There are few exceptions to this rule. One exception might be IRC Section 42 (affordable housing program) and the tax credits it offers. Other possible exceptions might be certain types of qualified energy programs. But as an operating rule of thumb, investments should be made for their economic potential, with income tax considerations as an ancillary part of the decision process.

Another helpful general rule is that there is usually a corollary between tax benefits and loss of liquidity. For example, an investment in an annuity usually enjoys tax-deferred status on any subsequent gain. However, any distribution from that annuity prior to age fifty-nine and a half will be treated as earnings-out-first, and the gain will be subject to a 10% tax penalty. So much for liquidity.

Numerous investments offer enticing income tax advantages. When properly arranged, for example, annuities and life insurance encounter no income tax on the gain in the contract cash value until there is a distribution. This tax advantage is referred to as *tax deferral*. Municipal bonds are generally free of federal income tax, and may also be free of state income tax. The dividends on these investments are then said to be *tax exempt*. As pointed out earlier, an investment in a properly managed section 42 affordable-housing program may offer *tax credits*. Tax credits are the most powerful tax advantage, since each dollar of credit reduces by one dollar your tax liability.

One of the most common mistakes in this area is to equate a tax benefit with the underlying investment. For example, I've heard people say they would not invest in an IRA again, because it had a poor rate of return. In fact, the portion of the tax code that authorizes Individual Retirement Accounts (IRAs) distinctly lists the types of investments that may qualify for this special tax advantage. A mutual fund might be categorized as tax exposed (meaning any dividends, interest, or capital gains would be taxable in the year they are earned), or tax deferred, in the case of an IRA. It might even be offered as a "separate account" in a variable annuity or a variable universal life contract, and qualify as tax deferred as a result. Be careful that you don't mistakenly assume that any special tax advantage that an investment receives is synonymous with the underlying investment itself.

Remember to Do the Math

In summary, as you approach the issue of developing an investment program, remember that the first step in the process is to do the math. First, determine how much you will need, when you will need it, and for what length of time. Then subtract your available income sources and determine your shortage. At this point, you can begin finding solutions for that need and begin considering different rates of return. Once this math is done, you can begin selecting appropriate investments that will best help you achieve your goals. Remember to search logically for the best investments to help you solve your investment goals and not to emotionally determine in advance whether you like a particular investment or not.

In this section, I've considered hypothetical examples and related it to retirement income. The same process should be used for any investment goal you may have, such as funding for a college education, a down payment on a home, or the dream of your own cabin in the woods.

The best advice on investment strategy that I can offer consists of the following:

1. If you have designed your financial plan specifically to support your life plan, then your investment decisions will always have the proper context. Just like a puzzle, if you don't know what the picture is supposed to look like, whatever piece you pick up and try to "fit" will not match the intended outcome.

2. Remember that there are many types of risk that can be managed effectively through diversification

3. Don't ever believe that you, or anyone else, can ever consistently predict the market. Common sense alone suggests that if that were possible, everybody would be doing it!

4. Always consider income tax consequences of any investment decision. Tax deductions and tax credits have the same effect as investment return. Whether you save $3,000 in taxes or you earn $3,000 on your investment, the result is the same.

5. Don't think you can ever know it all. It is always good to become more knowledgeable, but to get the most out of your financial resources, I strongly recommend that you seek professional advice.

CHAPTER 9

Good News
for Retirees

His assets totaled almost $1 million. On top of that, he had a pension of almost $3,000 a month, Social Security, and rental property income. He and his wife were about seventy years old and not in the best of health. As we talked during an annual review, I looked at Jack McGrueger and said, "Jack, in reviewing your financial plan, I have uncovered a real problem."

Jack's face took on a grim countenance. "Oh, what's that?" he said.

"You don't spend enough money!"

Retirees, in general, do have a problem. They tend to not spend enough money—which is really counterintuitive. Individuals in this age category many times live like paupers. In the financial planning process, there are two distinct dimensions—accumulation and distribution. One is used while you are a wage earner and the other is used as you move into retirement. There is a tendency at every age to focus on the *accumulation phase*—where the objective is to save, earn higher returns on your investments, and pay less taxes. Throughout life, people apply so much effort toward the goal of accumulation that, typically, when it comes time in life to change to distribution, they struggle and almost feel as if they are violating some ethical principle. This phase gets so ingrained into people—particular those individuals who have grown up during or immediately following the Great Depression—that accumulation ends up becoming the goal for life!

Retirees who have a hard time moving to the *distribution phase* of financial planning fail to appreciate that money is only a facility for supporting life goals. Prudent financial planning is not just about accumulating money. By now, you know that *Money for Life* is an effort to help people understand that money is nothing more than sustenance for life. Think of money in terms of the air you breathe: You need it to sustain you throughout life. If you were, say, playing basketball, you'd find that your body would require substantial volumes, sometimes in gasps. But while sleeping, you don't require tremendous volumes, since your system is relaxed. So it is also with money. Whatever amount you need better be there when you need it, or your life goals will suffer. The problem with many retirees is that they become so convicted over the years about the need to accumulate money that the idea of accumulation ends up becoming the goal itself. Instead of using their hard-earned accumulation to sustain a life of purpose during retirement, they continue to sock away more money into their savings. In the context of our metaphor, that is like having enough air to play basketball, but being afraid to use it. As a result, many retirees end up sleeping through their retirement.

Seniors tend to guard their wealth because of an underlying fear that if they are not careful their resources will disappear. Yet, if these retirees were simply to use the same prudent financial planning principles that permitted their financial success in the first place, they would realize that they could also successfully manage the distribution. Through prudent management, they will be able to have their money work for them in retirement, just as it did in prior years. Although successfully mastering this dimension requires a different strategy, the principle is exactly the same in effect—determine what you want for your life and develop the appropriate financial retirement plan to support it.

As I challenge retirees to commit to an appropriate distribution plan, I use a type of code language that means "live life." I don't mean that the retiree should live a narcissistic, self-consumed lifestyle. Rather, I want them to think creatively. For example, when their local church presents a major $10,000 mission project to the congregation and asks for help with the funding, many retirees automatically and immediately remove themselves from consideration. They listen to the presentation, but in their mind they've already decided, "This does not apply to me." They don't respond in this manner because they lack spiritual commitment. Rather, they respond this way because they have a financial mind-set that doesn't acknowledge that they have adequate financial resources. They protect their capital at all costs. In actuality, statistics show that many of these seniors do have the money for their church—and for a great deal of other beneficiaries, as well.

Whether you are a retiree or a young twenty-five-year-old, the same prudent financial principles apply. There are powerful, life-changing lessons in these principles for any age group. Fundamentally, the question remains the same: *What is your life plan?* Both ends of the age spectrum must continuously address this question.

Multidimensional Thinking for Retirees

Interestingly, for all the obvious differences between age groups, retirees tend to make the same mistake as their young counterparts do when it comes to planning their financial resources. Specifically, they buy CDs, invest in bonds, amass large amounts of equity in their home, and then look around to see what that produces for income. In essence, they allow their financial plan to dictate their life plan. They've put their (financial planning) cart before the (life) horse.

If retirees would first consider their life goals and then develop a financial plan to support that life (put the horse before the cart), they would feel so much more in control and find that life becomes ever more fulfilling.

The majority of financial planners take a fairly remedial risk-averse approach when it comes to investment recommendations for retirees. They fall into the same trap as their clients—they propose the overriding goal of protecting the nest egg at all costs.

Let me be clear that I am *not* suggesting that anyone jeopardize his nest egg. Rather, my suggestion is to first consider the retiree's dreams for life—almost as if money were no object—before committing to a particular financial strategy. For example, if everything in life were free, what would the retiree do with his next twenty-five years—or from age sixty-five to age ninety? If you can get the retiree to dig deep and to answer this question honestly, then the financial plan will begin to take shape. The point of the exercise is to suspend thoughts about money and instead focus on what he wants to do with his life.

This thought process takes time—sometimes days, weeks, or months. What does he want to do with his life for the next twenty-five years? The financial planner must wait until he answers this question. Then and only then will the planner be able to help arrange the retiree's financial portfolio to accomplish support for this life plan.

For example, a retiree is successful and has accumulated $750,000 by age seventy for a nest egg. At this point, his home is completely paid (or almost paid) and it requires a low monthly maintenance. Between his pension and Social Security, he is able to pay his monthly expenses.

If $750,000 were invested in bank instruments (certificates of deposit) earning 4.5%, interest earnings would equal $33,750 a year. Instead of bank instruments, what if he used the same approach that created the $750,000—or an appropriate asset allocation using a combination of mutual funds and variable annuities. If he were able to get a 12% return, his income would jump to $90,000 a year, or a difference of $56,250 a year. These figures are not based on historical data and should be interpreted only as a hypothetical scenario. Always consult the prospectus for specific fund history prior to making any investments. Without adjusting for inflation, if that person is going to live for another twenty-five years, it's a difference of $1,406,250— almost $1.5 million—and the principal investment of $750,000 is not touched. Would this person make different life choices if he knew at the conclusion of the financial planning process that somebody would walk in the door and hand him a check for $1.4 million? You lose opportunity and money if you create your financial plan without a life plan and instead allow the financial plan to dictate your life choices.

About six years ago, Mary Adams came into my office with a hodgepodge of a financial plan—really no plan at all. Two years before our meeting, her husband had died; she had some mutual funds with a stockbroker in Chicago, a couple of annuities, some CDs, and a large amount of money in her checking account. When we started the process, her goal was to organize her financial junk drawer into a cohesive plan. As we went through the financial planning process described in Chapter 1, eventually we managed to double what she anticipated for her monthly income. As we rearranged her investment allocation, she was astounded that her income could be that high. She could not fathom that her income could increase from $2,000 a month to $4,000 a month simply through rearranging her assets into a coordinated portfolio.

During the first year of this new plan, Mary maintained her same spending habits and the additional income accumulated in her investment portfolio so that it grew at an even faster rate. In the second year of the program, Mary could see the reality of her increased income because it was accounted for on confirmation statements and annual reports.

One day I was in a staff meeting and my assistant interrupted. "Mary is on the phone, and it is fairly urgent that she talks with you right now if you can make it." I left the meeting and thought something serious might have happened to Mary.

On the phone, Mary explained, "I'm visiting my grandchildren in a city about two hours away. This past week, I've had a difficult time squeezing my grandchildren into my small car."

On a whim, Mary stopped into a car dealership and fell in love with a van. "Right now, Stephen, my five grandchildren are climbing all over this van. The salesman says this van is a great vehicle for a grandmother. You told me that I could spend more money, and I want to buy this van. Do I have enough money?"

Her enthusiasm dripped through the phone, and I laughed with her, "Absolutely, Mary. Buy the van."

I don't want to give the impression that everyone can always raise his standard of living simply by rearranging an investment portfolio. That's foolish. Rather, my point is that for the most part, retirees tend to use outdated financial strategies that may have worked well in the 1930s, 1940s, 1950s, and even the 1960s. But today, the financial landscape looks entirely different from what it did back then. Just as technology, improvements in health services, transportation, and a host of other areas of life have benefited retirees, so, too, can state-of-the-art portfolio management.

One of the easiest ways to move toward this improvement without taking on substantial risk is to move from bonds and CDs to asset allocation using mutual funds, individual stocks and bonds in a wrap account, or a variable annuity. If your financial planner doesn't have adequate technology to help you manage your investment portfolio using asset allocation principles generally referred to as Modern Portfolio Theory on a real time, dynamic basis, I recommend you change financial planners. But it's your choice. Just like our earlier example, you, too, can choose to have either $33,000 a year or $90,000 a year.

The Trust Factor

One of the saddest facts about dealing with retirees—particularly those individuals in their seventies, eighties, and nineties—is the inherent lack of trust they generally have. Many people who fall into this age bracket absolutely refuse to share anything about their financial situation with the family. The consequences of this lack of financial information for the family are multiple and geometric, and go beyond just financial issues.

If you don't inform your family about your financial matters, when you die they won't have a clue whether you even had any financial resources, where to find those financial resources, how they were titled, and how to process them. Many times people find out this information in Probate Court. This lack of information creates all sorts of problems and difficulties that transcend the financial.

When I was in Colorado, I went to see a young family on a ranch. I was working for a Lutheran financial services company, and this family had a file with the company. I decided to meet them. From the files, I saw a number of people—in fact, four different families—in this region with the last name of Krueger. So I asked, "Are you related to the other Kruegers?" It was a pretty safe guess—they lived in the same county, they were members of the same church, and their last name was the same.

After a long pause, the thirty-five-year-old head-of-the-household farmer sat down with a deep sigh and said, "Yes, they are my siblings. I have three brothers who are married and have children." He had no smile on his face; rather, he was frowning. He continued, "But we don't talk with them."

I wasn't sure what to do with that information and didn't follow it for elaboration. Over the ensuing months I got to know the Kevin Kruegers as I helped them with their financial and estate planning. I learned they owned a fourth of a previously undivided large original family farm. Kevin Krueger wanted to pass this land along to their children, which included a son and three girls. The children were too young at that point to appreciate the estate planning elements or to know if they would want to be farmers. Because of Kevin Krueger's experience with dividing an estate, he wanted his children's inheritance to be handled in a more efficient manner than his inheritance from his parents had been.

Kevin Krueger's motivation came from a family fiasco about five years previous. Their parents, who were in their late seventies, died suddenly in an automobile accident. These parents had not done any estate planning. In a simple will, the parents left the entire 35,000 acres on an undivided basis to the four sons who helped work the farm. Now they had a new problem—how would four families work the same farm? Who would divide it? Who would divide it with the greatest degree of fairness?

Because they were members of the same family and were all Christians, they decided to have a big family meeting. Kevin Krueger was the estate executor, so he prepared the details for the meeting. He came with a recommendation of how to divide the farm. He based his recommendation on land utilization, water rights, and those types of considerations. Everyone was in agreement that his plan made the most sense.

The next question to be determined was more specific. Which person should own which portion of the estate? Kevin had a recommendation about this, as well. Everyone at the meeting agreed his suggestion made a lot of sense. His recommendation catered to the specific interests of each sibling.

Within a week, however, Kevin got a letter from one brother's attorney. The letter stated the brother had decided against accepting that parcel and instead wanted a different parcel. In the interest of accommodating the family, Kevin said OK, but the other brother involved in the exchange did not agree with the change. This type of swapping and disagreement went on until an attorney represented every sibling. Everyone was threatening everyone else with a lawsuit.

Over the years, the courts finally settled the entire estate. In the end, no one got what he thought should have been his portion—and no one was speaking to the others. Sadly, this is a true story.

How can you prevent such a situation from happening in *your* family? As uncomfortable as it may be for the children, I recommend that the children approach the parents. Be blunt and say things like, "We need to talk about how you are going to transfer your estate upon your death. You need to tell me your wishes so I can make sure those wishes are honored."

The Importance of Inheritance

"A good man leaves an inheritance for his children's children, but a sinner's wealth is stored up for the right-eous" (Proverbs 13:22). *Strong's Concordance of the*

Bible lists 237 verses of Scripture that contain the word *inheritance*. In comparison, only 96 verses have the word *forgiven* or *forgive* in them. This comparison provides insight into God's concept of inheritance.

The material that we accumulate on this earth will only be used to glorify God in the next generation if we protect it through developing an appropriate estate-transfer program. There are almost countless ways your estate may be eroded after your death, most especially through taxes. Most often, this situation can be mitigated with an effective transfer process—which is put in place before death.

The most popular means to transfer wealth through inheritance is through a will. In its most basic form, the will is a letter of instructions, which is usually administered through the state Probate Court system. Although many states have improved on this process through making it less time-consuming and expensive, still the time and expense can add a great deal to the survivors' stress and frustration. However, the situation is even worse when the deceased fails to leave a will. In these situations, the Probate Court administers something called the laws of intestacy. In fact, if you die without a will, then the state uses a statute to dictate the distribution of your possessions. The survivors' grief and frustration is compounded through intestacy, which could have been avoided entirely with proper planning.

One way people are addressing the concerns of cost, time, and lack of privacy in the management and transfer of an estate is through a living trust. This process begins the estate management process while the parties are still alive. Their assets are transferred to the trust. When compared to making a simple will, establishing a living trust often involves some additional effort, time, and expense. Yet at the time of death or of cognitive disability, there will be considerably less hassle, cost, and frustration because a trust would not be subject to the Probate Court process. My suggestion is to consult with a financial planner and attorney to determine whether a will or a living trust would be most appropriate for your particular situation.

Another item you will need to address is the living will. This document establishes your wishes regarding life support systems. Before signing such a document, you will want to consult family and your pastor for proper counsel.

Estate Taxes

While a thorough review of the unified transfer tax (estate and gift tax) is beyond the scope of this book, we should examine it briefly. Be aware that unless you have a properly constructed will, which includes a Credit Shelter Trust, you may be positioning your family for a severe estate tax at a later date. Each citizen is allowed to use tax credits that equal an equivalent exemption of between \$675,000* and \$1 million, depending on the year of the death. In other words, every person may pass up to \$675,000* in assets to others. The problem arises when a couple decides to use the unlimited marital deduction and one spouse passes the entire value of his or her portion of the estate to the surviving spouse.

When the transfer is made this way, it effectively eliminates the opportunity to apply the otherwise available tax credits to the decedent's portion of the combined estate. Over time, it may be that the real estate, savings, retirement account, business, stock, and other property in the decedent's estate combined with the survivor's portion will exceed \$675,000*. At this point, there may be federal estate tax liability on any portion exceeding that \$675,000*. Keep in mind the minimum tax rate begins at 37% and goes all the way up to 55% as a result of the tax law that President Bill Clinton signed after his 1992 election. When combined with state inheritance tax, income tax, and any excess accumulation, tax or excise tax, it is possible the ultimate beneficiaries may receive well below 25 cents on each dollar! Consider such matters the next time you go to the polls.

The obvious approach to this problem is to plan. You should plan your investments so you won't trigger excise, or excess accumulation taxes. Use financial

---

*26 USC Sec. 2057

strategies that reduce the ultimate impact of income taxes. And above all, make sure through proper planning that you are positioned to take full advantage of any tax credits that you can use.

Preventive Maintenance—Retirees and Estate Planning

Part of my recommendation to retirees involves working with an estate planning attorney—not just any attorney, but one who specializes in estate planning.

With the attorney, make sure you discuss two things in particular:

1. *A Credit Shelter Trust that will maximize the amount of the estate to be passed on upon death without incurring federal estate taxes.* This trust is designed to take full advantage of tax credits that you are entitled to.

2. *A living trust that is very efficient, private, and cost-effective way to transfer an estate upon death.* A living trust will not affect taxes.

The traditional method for transferring assets upon death is to use the Probate Court system. The instrument to be used within that system is called a will. The Probate Court system is a public process, so there is no way to keep matters private. Also, Probate Court is an expensive process because you have not only court costs but also attorneys' fees, which generally amount to 2% to 5% of the value of the estate.

The traditional method is also time consuming. In many cases it takes years. The whole process invites counterclaims from people who may want to get part of the estate. Some of these people might hire an "ambulance chaser" attorney on a contingency basis to see what the attorney can accomplish.

In a fashion completely opposite to the public, expensive, and inefficient Probate Court process, the living trust is used for transferring the estate. Living trusts are revocable (which means the person creating the trust can change his or her mind any time on any variable while he is alive). A living trust does not have any income tax or estate tax implications in and of itself. A living trust is private and efficient. Upon the death of the grantor, the trustee of the trust simply shows a particular financial institution a letter of instruction that is associated with the trust regarding the disposition of the property. It is no more complicated than showing the proper letter to the proper person after death. There are no attorneys beyond creating the living trust in the first place. No court appearance is required.

A living trust is particularly advantageous when you have property in multiple states because otherwise a

Probate Court experience would be required in each separate state where there is property.

Sometimes when it comes to legal documents such as handling matters of our estate, we are penny-wise and pound-foolish. A will today can be written as inexpensively as a $75 purchase of a software program. Or the family attorney can write the will for $150 to $250. The living trust is probably going to cost between $1,500 and $3,000. However, if the living trust is executed properly, it will include the Credit Shelter Trust and all other estate management instruments required in order to maximize the efficient transfer of the estate upon death.

The cost of a living trust may be more expensive on the front end, but it costs virtually nothing later. This is in contrast to the will that must be continuously updated by adding codicils anytime there is a marriage, birth, or additional property, and that continuously involves attorneys. In the final analysis, it costs much less to use a living trust than it does to use a simple will to transfer your estate.

Within the financial planning industry, we understand how attorneys love wills and often refer to wills as the their own private annuity. They write a will for someone who is sixty, and they recognize that during the next thirty years, they will be able to convert that will to a Probate Court experience. They assume that since they wrote the original will, the family will return to them for the Probate

Court process (at a considerably greater cost). In general, attorneys don't like living trusts because after they write the document, their role is over. Any changes that need to be made because of births or additional property can be handled without their involvement.

Why Inheritance Is Important

Scripture has an emphasis on inheritance for a reason—to remove our apathetic attitude about this issue. If we remain apathetic about it, then it is ultimately selfish—since-I-can't-take-it-with-me-then-I-don't-care attitude. But according to the Bible, we should care. The Lord isn't finished with us when we are finished. His purpose, His ministry, and His truth live on. Our selfishness and callousness is exposed when we don't glorify the Lord through the preservation of our material wealth. Properly cared for, His purpose on earth will benefit through our planned generosity.

A few years ago, I was asked by a pastor friend of mine to help him manage some inheritance that he was going to receive from his parents' estate. As part of this process, we discussed his estate plan. "How do you want your money distributed upon your death?" I asked him. He thought a minute and then answered, "I suppose it should be divided equally among my living children." I was quite surprised by his answer since it did not make any provision for the church or for any mission or outreach program. After all, I had known this pastor to be both crippled in his efforts at ministry because of lack of financial resources and at the same time forceful in his preaching about the responsibility we have to give.

If it is true that we don't own anything while we are alive, but instead simply manage what God entrusts to us, it is certainly true that we don't own anything when we die. Yet most Christians' giving habits during their life, lacking though they may be, considerably outweigh their giving upon death. If we are expected to give of the firstfruits while living, doesn't it make sense to do at least that much with our estate assets upon death?

CHAPTER 10

Flex Your
Political Muscle

It was a spring morning in Colorado in 1986. I was lying awake in bed, enjoying the aroma of coffee coming from the kitchen. My mind wandered to thoughts about the day. Where should I go? What should I do? Well, let's see. I could grab a couple of horses and head up to the mountains for a ride. I could go for a run, catch a quick shower, and then head to a ball game. Or I could go to work. What an odd set of choices, I thought. It was Wednesday, and I was actually thinking about playing hooky from work? I'm not an undisciplined sort of guy. I like my work, and I believe in a good work ethic. So why was I thinking about doing something other than work?

I had been blessed. My career in financial services had taken off. Of course, I paid a price for that success. Long hours, the risk of a new career, a lot of schooling, a move halfway across country. But it was paying off. I was earning more money now than I had ever dreamed of. But the problem was, I didn't get to keep much of it. In fact, as I lay there in bed, it occurred to me that I got to keep 45 cents for every dollar I made! Now, that's motivation! I could go to work and apply myself with my best skill and give the government 55 cents, and keep 45 cents for my family. Nah, I think I'll pass. I've earned enough for this month. I'll enjoy myself today instead of going to work.

It is impossible to think about developing a financial plan to support a life plan without also thinking about the government. What a sad commentary that is. But it is true. The government forces investment decisions to become twisted in order to reduce income taxes. Loved ones are forced to cough up part of the family's estate so that government can "redistribute" it to others. Financial decisions today are not made based only on their economic merit, but rather on their "tax consequences." As absurd as this is, government keeps right on getting away with it. Why do Americans allow more of their money to go to the government now than at any other time in history? I think that if you approached one of the original Minutemen and told him that 200 years later his family would have to pay more to the federal government in taxes than his family would spend on food, clothing, and shelter combined, he would either laugh at you or grab you by the collar and take you to the authorities as a traitor. Oh how far we have come. The reason late twentieth-century Americans seem ambivalent about the bite that government takes can be attributable to "the frog" phenomenon.

Like a Frog in a Kettle

Here's a metaphorical question for you to consider: "How do you boil a frog?" Well, I can tell you that you don't boil a frog by heating a kettle of water until it boils and then throwing the frog into the pot. If you do, the frog will immediately jump out of the pot.

Rather, a frog is boiled by placing him in lukewarm water and slowly, over time, raising the temperature of the water, until the frog, enjoying his warmth, is overcome with the increased heat. He ends up being boiled. The same principle is true with taxation in America.

As you work with a financial planner and develop a plan for your life and your money, keep in mind that tax considerations are always an unfortunate component of the financial planning equation. What you will ultimately invest in will have almost as much to do with tax considerations as it will with the underlying economic viability of the investment. How absurd! And you'll find yourself asking how did our country get in such a situation, where the individuals pay such a large percentage of their income and earnings to their government? In the next few pages, I'm going to briefly explain the history, explore our national roots, and talk about what individuals can do to change the current situation.

Let's go back to the beginning. Our country hasn't always been this way. In fact, it has only been in this century that we have strayed from the course our forefathers intended. Our founding fathers were something more than just historical opportunists. Their convictions ran all the way to their very souls. Just take a moment and consider some of the sacrifices our forefathers made so that you and I could live free.

Have you ever wondered what happened to the fifty-six men who signed the Declaration of Independence? If you are like most Americans, the answer is probably no, because we so take for granted what they did. Well, here's the real story about American patriotism.* See if it doesn't reinvigorate your patriotism and commitment to those original American principals.

The British captured five signers as traitors, then tortured them before they died. Twelve signers had their homes ransacked and burned. Two signers lost sons who served in the Revolutionary Army, and two sons of another signer were captured. Nine signers fought and died from wounds or hardships of the Revolutionary War.

These men pledged their lives, their fortunes, and their sacred honor. What were their vocations?

---

*This information is accurate so far as I know.

Twenty-four were lawyers and jurists. Eleven were merchants; nine were farmers and large plantation owners. All were men of means and well educated. They signed the Declaration of Independence knowing full well that the penalty would be death if their government, the British, captured them.

Carter Braxton of Virginia, a wealthy planter and trader, saw his ships swept from the seas by the British navy. He sold his home and properties to pay his debts and died in rags.

British soldiers so hounded Thomas McKeam that he was forced to move his family almost constantly. He served in the Congress without pay, and his family was kept in hiding. His possessions were taken from him, and poverty was his reward. Vandals or soldiers looted the properties of Dillery, Hall, Clymer, Walton, Gwinnett, Heyward, Ruttledge, and Middleton.

At the battle of Yorktown, Thomas Nelson Jr. noted that British General Cornwallis had taken over the Nelson home for his headquarters. He quietly urged General George Washington to open fire. The home was destroyed, and Nelson died bankrupt.

Francis Lewis had his home and properties destroyed. The enemy jailed his wife, and she died within a few months.

John Hart was driven from his wife's bedside as she was dying. Their thirteen children fled for their lives. His fields and his gristmill were laid to waste. For more than a year he lived in forests and caves, returning home to find his wife dead and his children vanished. A few weeks later he died from exhaustion and a broken heart. Norris and Livingston suffered similar fates.

Such were the stories and sacrifices of the American Revolution. These were not wild-eyed, rabble-rousing ruffians. They were soft-spoken men of means and education. They had security, but they valued liberty more.

Standing tall, straight, and unwavering, they pledged: "For the support of this declaration, with firm reliance on the protection of the divine providence, we mutually pledge to each other, our lives, our fortunes, and our sacred honor."

They gave you and me a free and independent America. The history books never told you a lot of what happened in the Revolutionary War. We didn't just fight the British. We were British subjects at that time, and we fought our own government! Some of us take these liberties so much for granted. We shouldn't.

The Historical Roots of Our Taxation

Most Americans living today don't understand that provision for income taxes and estate taxes was not made in the United States Constitution. In fact, for the majority of the time that the United States have been a nation, our citizens never had to pay either estate taxes or income taxes. It wasn't until 1913 that Congress proposed the concept of taxing the wages of American citizens. Even then, the rhetoric in Congress promised that the rate of taxation from the government would never exceed 2%! Today that rate exceeds 40% when you consider the impact of the loss of deductions and exemptions combined with the highest marginal tax bracket.

Another egregious tax is the estate tax, which most people don't even consider. It doesn't affect them until a loved one dies—especially a relative with an excess of $625,000 in his estate. Estate taxes were first proposed in 1916. One of the reasons for enacting estate tax legislation was "to redistribute wealth." If that concept is not un-American, then I don't know what is. The congressmen who passed that law based their decision on the concept that those who have possessions should be taken from to give to those who do not have (and may not deserve) possessions.

In the late 1930s when the first provision for Social Security was suggested, and the first bulletin about Social Security was circulated by the Franklin Roosevelt administration, there was never an intent (as evidenced by the bulletin) to provide meaningful guaranteed retirement income for all Americans. Rather, Social Security was intended to be an income replacement for those Americans who were in poverty and could not otherwise provide for themselves. Additionally, Social Security tax was never supposed to exceed 3% of gross total wages. Today it is more than 15% and it is still not enough!

And the greatest irony of all is that, even though the government has so mismanaged the money they have taken from citizens in an effort to provide guaranteed retirement income, there are now not enough funds to pay even the amount that they took away back to those who paid! And yet no one seems to want to hold the government responsible.

Now as politicians wrestle with how to solve this problem—both fiscally and politically—none of the proposals that they are suggesting is fair. For example, one proposal is that each person should be allowed to make his own investment decisions regarding a *small portion* of the money that the government confiscates for Social Security. And we are supposed to be *thankful* for that privilege? Why not be allowed the freedom to invest *all* it? After all, whose money is it, anyway?

It's one thing to demand that each citizen be responsible and have retirement income—even going so far as to require evidence that there is such an account. But for the government to forbid me, a financial planner—or money managers who manage billions of dollars or accountants, CPAs, or anyone else—from managing his own retirement money is the height of arrogance and autocracy. It shows the extent to which our government feels confident in playing with our money in order to buy votes.

What Can You Do to Fight This Injustice?

As you read this information, it may shock you. It's like a stream of cold water being poured over the frog at just the last moment. You may find yourself thinking, *This is ridiculous! I've never thought about it like this. But what can I—one person out of 250 million people—do?*

You can respond in the same way that Americans have responded throughout history. Become educated about these issues. Consider the various politicians who want to manage your money. Start with the presidential candidates, senators, congressmen, and governors. These people have the right to force you to give them part of your hard-earned money and part of your assets—on demand.

These leaders are the ones that you need to become well acquainted with. More important, you need to learn about their policies and their philosophy. If you do not subscribe to the idea that government should be the provider of guaranteed retirement income, health insurance, housing, and employment, then you should reflect on what Thomas Jefferson said almost two hundred years ago: "The best government is the government that governs least." Support those candidates who reflect that philosophy, particularly when it comes to income taxes, estate taxes, and the Social Security boondoggle.

Make sure that your voice is heard. With the Internet, it is easy to communicate with your elected officials. One of the many things I learned by attending the 1994 Campaign Management School presented by the Republican National Committee is that your voice is heard.

Make sure that your friends, your family, your church, and other organizations where you have affiliations are equally educated.

Be aware that if you do not make your life a direct reflection of your personal values, then all the resources that you have throughout your life, by default, will be used to support someone else's values.

That's why the United States' fiscal policy is out of control. We've been too complacent. But the water is getting pretty warm.

Here's a question for you. If instead of all those taxes going on a one-way trip to Washington, D.C., they went back into the U.S. economy, what would happen? What if $2 trillion were returned to the economy instead of applied to the national debt? After all, it is our money. And since you are a wage earner, a taxpayer, and a potential recipient of this "refund," what would you do with this money? Most likely, you would invest it, spend it, buy a home, send your children to a better college. The economic result would mushroom.

Yes, our economy is doing well, and we are still a great nation—the greatest nation on earth. The problem is, we are headed in the wrong direction.

Ronald Reagan used to say often, "This is still the American experiment." How long can we keep this thing going? There have been previous attempts at such experiments, but then dictators or revolutions again have prevented democratic republics from continuing to evolve. I don't foresee a revolution or major political upheaval in the short term. But I do see a continuation of the road that we've been going on. And this road is headed straight to socialism.

The bottom line is that the American dream, as fought for by our forefathers, was to enable you to have a full, free, unencumbered opportunity to reach your full potential. In order for this to be true, however, you also must (simultaneously) have the opportunity for failure.

If government is going to guarantee against the risk of failure, then you are going to have to take the cost of that guarantee out of your opportunity for success. When we started this country over 200 years ago, there was tremendous opportunity for failure and unbridled opportunity for success.

The American ideal began to crumble early in the twentieth century when we went from a country of transactional tax to a country of confiscatory tax. Eventually, even the states thought the idea of confiscatory tax a heyday, so they got in on the act. Finally, even municipalities found the idea too alluring to pass up. Now everyone is taxing you. It has become so ridiculous and unbridled that even after federal, state, and municipal taxes are levied, the few dollars you have remaining are then taxed by various government agencies on items such as fuel, "luxury" items, personal properties, and so forth. Is this the American dream?

You no longer have unbridled opportunity for success. You have limited opportunity for success. Why has this change happened? The government is now using the amount of success that you have forfeited to guarantee that no one fails. It is literally impossible for anyone to fail in this country.

If you live a normal life—obviously this statement doesn't include beggars in the street—and if you want to avail yourself of all the social services that exist, you need not produce any income. There are health benefits that are appropriated to you because you are an American citizen on both the federal and state level. There are retirement benefits appropriated to you because you are an American citizen. There are housing benefits that you can take advantage of because you are an American citizen. And if you happen to fall into a particular category of minority or are female, you have an even greater opportunity and increased access to these services. You may have opportunities in education that you wouldn't have otherwise if you have no money or are of a particular demographic group the government is courting.

It's almost impossible to fail in this country. If you get out of bed and you go to work, you are going to get Social Security and Medicare benefits and be able to avail yourself of some housing. You can't be discriminated against because you are a homosexual, are of a particular color, or are a female. All these distinctions have to be paid for and administered. Where does it come from? It comes from you. Your hard work, your risk, and your creativity. Please understand that the government does not create any money. Rather, the government takes from some in order to give to others—in an effort to stay in power. Our elected officials are a conduit of your money—that's all.

When a politician says, "We are going to give you a $500 tax credit so that you can send your child to college," everyone begins to applaud and talk about how they are going to support that politician. But when will people stop and realize that the money that politician is talking about "giving back" was yours in the first place! And now we applaud at the prospect of getting *some* of it back—and even then only if we qualify and use it the way government prescribes. It makes no sense.

Plato had it right. In Plato's *Republic,* he divided society into three groups—leaders, managers, and workers. When the combination of workers and managers reach a point where there are more of them than leaders, and when unscrupulous leaders figure out how to manipulate the masses for their own political benefit, the democracy fails.

I encourage you to stay awake. There is still time. Get involved. Don't get boiled.

CHAPTER 11

Adam walked into the house, satisfied with having just completed a successful campaign on behalf of the local Crisis Pregnancy Center. For a number of years, Adam had served on the board of the center after he had been convicted on the abortion issue as a teenager. He went "too far" with his girlfriend and she got pregnant.

For help, Adam prayed, talked with his pastor and, finally, his parents. Then he decided to marry his girlfriend and give the child a proper family. Unfortunately, his girlfriend had no interest in his marriage proposal. And, even more shocking to Adam, she also had no interest in carrying the child to term. Ever since *Roe* v. *Wade* changed the soul of America, the father of this unborn child had no rights. He had responsibility, to be sure. But only if the mother decided that she wanted to carry the child to term. In that case, whether the father agreed or not was of no consequence. On the one hand, the mother could order the father to pay child support and could even order a DNA test to prove her claim to his financial resources in perpetuity. On the other hand, she might just decide to end the pregnancy—again without regard to the father's wishes. So Adam sat helplessly as his girlfriend received counseling and then an abortion from the local Planned Parenthood facility.

Although that experience happened ten years ago, the memory still haunts Adam. He wonders what his child would have looked like, what he or she might have grown up to become. He grieves for the child that his girlfriend and her counselors aborted. Shortly thereafter, Adam decided to do everything in his power to support others who were suddenly in the frightening position of an unplanned pregnancy. He hoped that he could help them protect the life that they were given, whether convenient, or not.

One day Adam walked to the refrigerator and poured a diet soda while browsing through his unopened mail. One of the envelopes contained a quarterly report from a mutual fund company where Adam had a small IRA. He opened it and pulled out the contents. As usual, this report was filled with performance figures, a comprehensive report to shareholders from the fund manager, and his individual account statement. As he took a drink from his glass, Adam noticed a "Listing of Key Holdings" in the report. He about choked on his soda as he recognized one of the companies whose stock was held by his IRA mutual fund. It was a national company with high name recognition and one with strong ties to

Planned Parenthood. Adam couldn't believe it. Here he had devoted thousands of hours on a volunteer basis to promote life instead of abortion. Yet at the same time he was giving his investment dollars to a company who in turn gave financial support to Planned Parenthood, a business dedicated to abortion rights.

Suddenly Adam felt like a hypocrite, a fake, and an imposter. Also he felt like going to the phone and demanding an immediate redemption of all his money held in that mutual fund. But Adam had a problem. Before he could make the call to liquidate his investment in that fund, he first had to find out where he could invest his money in a mutual fund that would reflect his values and not Planned Parenthood's values. After all, it was *his money* and it should reflect *his values*. What assurance would he have that the next values-indiscriminate mutual fund wouldn't run the same risk?

Adam's story is not unique. Millions of investors each year face the same quandary. Many people have told me things like, "I watched my father die a horrible death from lung cancer after years of smoking. I don't care where you invest my money, I just don't want any of it to find its way into the tobacco industry."

What Is Values-Based Investing?

Values-based investing is the idea of allowing an investor the opportunity to align his or her values with his investments. Most people are unaware of the fact that some of the money that they invest in their IRAs or mutual funds or their retirement program might actually find its way into various stocks and bonds in companies whose business practices might be offensive to their personal values. These offenses would include abortion, pornography, gambling, and the advocacy of same-sex lifestyles. Unsuspectingly, most people who have investments in IRAs, mutual funds, and 401(k)s have their money in industries that are absolutely contrary to their values.

The idea of values-based investing is simply the idea that we add one nonfinancial question to the investment decision-making process: "Do you want your personal values reflected in your investment choices?"

How can you know if your 401(k) is invested in these companies? Until recently, there has not been a way to determine this values-based information. However, through the efforts of companies like the Values Investment Forum in Jackson, Mississippi, a great deal of research has been done over the last few years. VIF has combined efforts with other companies like Cornerstone Capital Management in Colorado Springs and the Values Financial Network in Nashville. Together they have provided a way for individuals to examine their investment portfolio to see exactly where their invested dollars end up.

You can get information about your mutual funds through two sources: Values Investment Forum and Values Financial Network.

Values Investment Forum. Call the Values Investment Forum in Jackson, Mississippi, 1-662-842-5033. Capable people there will help you find information. For example, if you tell them which mutual fund or subaccounts with a variable annuity or which mutual funds are in your 401(k), they can tell you to what extent your investments are in line with your personal values. They examine six issues: abortion, pornography, gambling, same-sex lifestyles, alcohol, and tobacco.

Values Financial Network. Log on to the Web site of the Values Financial Network: <http://www.vfn.com/>. Using state-of-the-art technology, the VFN offers the opportunity to any investor to screen his mutual funds, variable annuities, 401(k), or IRA in the privacy and comfort of his own home. An investor can discover the extent to which his investments hold stock in companies that are involved in alcohol, tobacco, gambling, pornography, abortion, or companies that support a same-sex lifestyle.

I suggest if you investigate your holdings. You may be shocked at the results.

Many times when we use the word *investments* people get glassy-eyed or bored. They tend to think of that word as meaning something very sophisticated and much beyond them. Yet almost everyone who works in the United States has some form of retirement plan—such as a 401(k) or, if they work for a church or public institution, a 403(b) or maybe an IRA. Or maybe they have savings plan for college and are using mutual funds. Every single one of those investments potentially has as much as 50 cents of every dollar invested in these six issues. This is a tremendous compromise of stewardship and values. In the majority of cases, the investors *don't even know* that this situation exists. They simply have never considered the idea.

I was asked recently. "Is it possible that my college savings for my daughter could be invested in stocks of companies involved in pornography or abortion or that promote a same-sex lifestyle?"

It is not only feasible, but it is also highly likely. Most mutual funds have some portion of their money invested directly into one or more of these six issues.

You may be asking, "What are my alternatives? I'm bothered by this information and I'm ready to do something about it. What can I do? What do you recommend to me?"

Your first step is to find out the condition of your investments in relation to your values. If you have an investment portfolio that is doing well for you, have the portfolio screened—every part of it, including your IRA, 401(k), mutual funds, and variable annuity. Let the

Values Investment Forum tell you whether your investments are in line with your values.

To the extent that they are not in line with your values, find some help. Hundreds of financial advisers across the country would be more than happy to help you find a way to create an investment portfolio that is similar in investment characteristics to what you have—and at the same time matches your personal values.

In my opinion, to live life with integrity, it is absolutely essential that everyone—whether Christian or not—makes sure everything in his or her life lines up with his values. To line your life with your values will mean taking a serious look at the people you associate with, the things that you do, the things that you talk about, the books that you read, the movies that you watch—and certainly the investments that you make. Integrating your values completely into your life would also certainly include the relationship you have with your family.

Promise Keepers, the men's movement that was started a decade ago by former Colorado football coach Bill McCartney and has since swept the nation, is a wonderful example of the practical application of personal values. Beginning with a focus on Christ as the redeemer of a fallen world and then moving to the apostle Paul's emphasis on love as the prime motivator for all that we do, Promise Keepers has helped educate millions of men of all ages and walks of life. If we think first about God's unrelenting, unconditional love for us as individuals as well as a community, we then find our values orientation that serves as the compass for directing all that we do we—with particular emphasis on family leadership and servitude.

The Values Financial Network has been a major sponsor of the Promise Keepers conferences. I remember being emotionally and spiritually moved as I watched men crowd around the VFN exhibit at the Denver event, trying to learn more about values-based investing. These men were convicted of the need to align everything in their lives with their values, and it was intuitive for them to know that money, beyond simply budgeting, was all too often not given proper scrutiny. The men gathered around the display, looking through the materials and listening to the presenters as they told their values-based investing story. It quickly become so cramped that many men simply elbowed their way through to tear off a piece of paper, scribble their name, and, as they handed it to one of the VFN members, say, "Please have someone call me. I need to evaluate my IRA and mutual funds."

The idea of aligning your money with your values is a relatively new concept in America. It is not, however, a new concept with Christ, who said, "Where your heart is, there your treasure will be too" (Matthew 6:21; Luke 12:34). Unfortunately, some Americans are so concerned with getting the "best" return that they never even stop to think how their money is being used. So long as their return is good, many simply don't care.

Let's reevaluate this concept of a good return no matter what the cost. Imagine that you've gone back almost 2,000 years and are walking along the shores of Galilee with Jesus and his disciples. You listen as they plan the next few days and consider travel distance, personnel, and resources. Jesus calls to his treasurer (He did in fact have one) and asks, "How are we doing?"

His treasurer responds, "Master, I have great news. We are doing quite well. In fact, we've just earned a quick 25% on our last investment."

At that, Jesus stops and turns to his treasurer and asks, "Twenty-five percent? That is good. But tell me, where did you find an investment opportunity like that?"

His treasurer responds, "Well, you know that new brothel in lower Jerusalem, with all the international traffic coming through, and all the religious festivals? Their business is booming!"

Now, let me ask you. If that scenario had occurred, do you think Jesus would have: (a) given his treasurer a high-five, or (b) severely rebuked him, and told him to go and immediately pull their money out.

The answer is obvious.

You might be thinking that this doesn't apply to you. After all, you certainly wouldn't *knowingly* invest in a brothel! Of course you wouldn't. And you probably would not knowingly invest in any company that published pornographic literature or made pornographic movies. And neither would you invest in pharmaceutical companies that manufacture chemicals called abortifacients, which are used to induce abortions. And if a representative of the Federation of Gay Games came to your door soliciting financial support for the gay and lesbian Olympic-style competition, you probably would turn them down. The problem, though, is that the companies who do provide that financial support are often supported themselves by mutual funds. And you do buy mutual funds. The company stock that is sold to them creates cash for expansion, operations, marketing, new products, and philanthropy.

The popularity of mutual funds has risen so dramatically in the last couple of decades that without an attitude of stewardship on your part, more than likely your hard-earned investment dollars do, in fact, find their way into these industries, making you a de facto financial contributor to them.

What Is True Stewardship?

There have been many different uses for the word *stewardship,* particularly in the Christian community. For the purpose of this book, I'll use the definition that is promoted by the Values Financial Network: Stewardship 1-2-3!

Stewardship 1 refers to the idea that everyone should have a financial plan to provide for life's challenges, care for the family, and be prepared for the future. That concept is both practical and scriptural. The apostle Paul wrote in his first letter to Timothy, "But those who won't care for their own relatives, especially those living in the same household, have denied what we believe. Such people are worse than unbelievers" (1 Timothy 5:8 NLT).

Stewardship 2 refers to the admonition to invest your money where your values are. To the extent that your beliefs and values go one direction but your money goes the other, you do not have the joy of living your life in alignment. Instead, you are like the "double-minded man" of the Bible (James 1:8), who can't make progress in life because he is constantly compromising himself. Investing your money in mutual funds, annuities, insurance, and so forth that specifically promote your values allows you a peace of mind associated with both financial security as well as a moral return on your invested assets.

Stewardship 3 refers to the concept of leveraging your money for the benefit of others. If there is anything more fundamental to Christian stewardship than using one's own resources for the betterment of others, I don't know what it would be. There are many opportunities to use money cleverly so that others benefit. These ways include giving to charity or tithing your income, or using a certain Visa card or money market account because it generates revenue to Promise Keepers, Habitat for Humanity, or Women of Faith.

Stewardship is much deeper than simply giving to charity or watching that you don't overspend. True stewardship involves every aspect of your life. Where you invest your money is an important part of the whole stewardship process. Since the idea of aligning one's money with one's values is becoming such a popular investment strategy, let's take a closer look at Stewardship 2.

To the extent that you either loan money to companies through bonds or give money to companies through investment in stocks through the purchase of mutual funds, you are literally helping these companies advance their business. Many of these companies have a values system that is totally opposite to yours.

For example, on the abortion issue, to the extent that a company is a big donor to Planned Parenthood—and there are many such companies—you have effectively enabled that company to use your money to support them. Your money, then, is enabling Planned Parenthood to support more abortions. That is an indisputable fact. I believe this information is critical for people to consider as they invest their money.

There is more at stake than just the returns on your investments. For example, who is going to benefit from the money involved in the investment? This question is also a decisive part of the investment decision. Until recently this information was not readily available. Thankfully, it is today. And it will become even more a part of the investment decision-making process in the future.

For perspective, let's consider for a moment what has been happening on the liberal side of the political question of investing with values. Remember the concern that companies had about investing in South Africa during apartheid? They pulled their investments from South Africa. You might also be aware of the fact that many companies fail environmental screening. Many mutual funds, private investment accounts, as well as church accounts refuse to invest in companies that have a poor environmental record. There is nothing wrong with this, but why be concerned only with these social issues? Aren't issues such as abortion and pornography even more important, particularly to social conservatives?

So just where is the conservative side of the values-based investment movement? There is over $3 trillion invested in what is labeled Socially Responsible Investments. SRI has been around for 20 years. But SRI represents the socially liberal investor. Socially conservative investors have amassed less than $500 million. We have been remiss in our own stewardship, and we can take a lesson from the liberal side of the political spectrum. They have lined their investment dollars with their values—and we can do the same.

Mutual funds have been one of the most important financial developments in the history of economics. Since the first mutual fund was organized in 1924, trillions of dollars have been invested, taking advantage of the diversification, liquidity, and professional management they offer. They are so popular today that mutual fund offerings outnumber available stocks on the New York Stock Exchange by almost four to one! In the last fifteen years, they have revolutionized the pensions and retirement plans of millions of people. Mutual funds are offered as the most popular options for the millions of working Americans who participate in their employer's 401(k) and 403(b) plans. Mutual funds are the preferred investment option for most Individual Retirement Accounts (IRAs). Beginning in the late 1980s, mutual fund type investments (technically referred to as *separate accounts*) began appearing in annuity and life insurance contracts as variable annuities and variable universal life policies. In less than a decade, variable annuities (and their mutual fund investments) have amassed over $868 billion.

As discussed earlier, you may be of the opinion that if you don't know where your money goes, then you aren't really responsible. In other words, if you do prudent research into investment options and decide on a particular mutual fund, then whatever stock that fund manager decides to purchase is not a matter for your personal stewardship. This kind of thinking (head-in-the-sand approach) is misguided.

Let's look at it another way. We are told that "Where your treasure is, there your heart will be also." Few parents would argue that, beyond the love they have for God, their hearts are always first with their children. Our children represent part of our treasure, and we therefore take great care with them.

If we followed the head-in-the-sand logic referenced earlier, we might think something like this: We are responsible for giving our children a proper home, love, and counsel. But when our sixteen-year-old asks for the car keys, it is not our responsibility to know where he goes, since he will no longer be in our home. Instead, we "turn them over to the car," and wherever they go in that car is not of any concern to us. We are no longer responsible when that "treasure" walks out of our sight. Nonsense! We have an uninterrupted, continuous stewardship responsibility.

Our secular, socially liberal investment peers have been much better at this investment stewardship issue than have those of us who hold to traditional American values.

This values-based aspect of the financial industry is growing rapidly. According to Weisenberger of Rockville, Maryland, assets invested in values-based funds rose from $1.5 billion in 1989 to $4.5 billion in 1998, faster than all other funds. And virtually all this growth is attributable to socially liberal investors who are not concerned with pornography, abortion, or keeping a same-sex agenda out of the workplace. Rather, the socially liberal investors are concerned with animal rights, the military industrial complex, and homosexual rights in the workplace.

Values-based (socially conservative values, that is) investing is part of the $3 trillion Socially Responsible Investing industry. With the advent of technology, mutual funds are quickly becoming transparent, allowing shareholders their first real glimpse at their holdings. For the first time, investors are becoming alarmed and are looking for appropriate alternatives.

The customer profile questionnaire that is fast becoming the new standard includes the question of the new millennium, "Would you like your personal values reflected in your investment program?" Through asking this one simple question, brokers will find out that their customer relationships become stronger, more meaningful, and longer lasting. Customers appreciate when a broker cares about them, and what better way to express that concern that by including the customer's values in the investment decision-making process.

The popularity of Socially Responsible Investing has mushroomed since it began in the 1920s. According to Tom Kee, writer for *BWZine,* the number of mutual and money market funds that use some type of social screening has increased from half a dozen in the early 1980s to over sixty in 1995. Today there are well over a hundred socially responsible funds.

I want to briefly comment on the most common misconception about values-based investing. Contrary to popular belief, you don't need to sacrifice a good return to invest your money in funds that are filtered by ethical criteria. According to Lloyd Kurtz, financial analyst at Harris, Bretall, Sillivan, and Smith, who has done a risk-adjusted analysis of the Domini Social Index, "All the research I've done shows social screens have no effect on performance." Earlier this year, the Domini Social Equity Fund made some history when it became the second social investment fund to pass the $1 billion mark. This news makes Domini the ninth fastest growing family fund in the nation, according to Domini Social Investments. The first such fund to reach $1 billion was Dreyfus Third Century, achieving its milestone in December 1998, according to Craig Tolliver at CBS Marketwatch.

I am pleased that so many people want their investments to reflect their personal values, regardless of their theological or political persuasion. What is disconcerting is that virtually all that investment growth has been invested using a socially liberal screen for such issues as animal rights, nuclear power, the military industrial complex, and minority preferences. Even the sweatshop issue is screened in some investments. As Joe Keefe, executive vice president at Citizen's Funds said, "Five years ago, there was no sweatshop screening, but that's becoming a more and more important issue." Moreover, he says, a lot of attention is also being paid to environmental sustainability and community investment. "These screens are evolving."

While the first SRI fund was developed in the early 1970s (for socially liberal investors), the first fund for socially conservative investors didn't appear until 1991. Those on the liberal side of the political spectrum have really beaten us out of the blocks. There is a mutual fund developed specifically for those who want to promote a homosexual lifestyle (Meyers Pride Fund). There is a bank that was formed to provide services to the gay and lesbian community (G & L Bank). There is even a national real estate referral service developed specifically for homosexuals. It is ironic that the issue of stewardship, such a traditional hallmark of the Christian community, has become so popular with secular liberals and in such short supply with Christians.

A problem of education exacerbates this disparity between the amount of money invested in socially liberal versus socially conservative funds. According to one report, socially conservative investors in SRI funds have invested at least $49 billion, because they thought they were investing in a fund that did, in fact, reflect their values. I remember interviewing a thirty-five-year-old member of my church for an executive level position not too long ago. The applicant and I were discussing values-based investing, a core component of Shepherd Financial Services' business.

When I explained that much of the money being used to support companies that support abortion, pornography, and a same-sex lifestyle actually came from evangelical Christians, he grew a wide smile and quipped, "Not me. My investments are in a mutual fund that screens out those issues."

I knew he was misinformed, but I wanted to let him make the discovery with me. So I connected to our Internet Web site and looked up the Washington Mutual Fund. Sure enough, it was listed as an SRI fund. It did screen out alcohol and tobacco, but it was also a major purchaser of stock in companies involved in (you guessed it!) abortion, pornography, and supporting a gay lifestyle. I looked away from the screen and toward him and saw his smile turn upside down.

With the combination of advanced and affordable technology, and with the increasing investor awareness of the values-choice option for their investment portfolio, things have begun to change. Today, there are about twenty mutual fund options for social conservatives, some of which utilize the skilled management of highly successful firms such as Templeton Portfolio Advisory Services, Nicholas Applegate, and Potomac. More are on the way. There are also investment advisory services devoted entirely to managing funds according to traditional values. Insurance companies have also gotten into the game, developing variable annuities and variable life products specifically for the socially conservative investor.

Figure 11-1

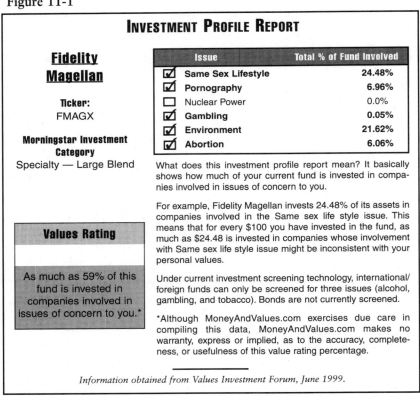

	Issue	Total % of Fund Involved
☑	Same Sex Lifestyle	24.48%
☑	Pornography	6.96%
☐	Nuclear Power	0.0%
☑	Gambling	0.05%
☑	Environment	21.62%
☑	Abortion	6.06%

INVESTMENT PROFILE REPORT

Fidelity Magellan

Ticker:
FMAGX

Morningstar Investment Category
Specialty — Large Blend

Values Rating

As much as 59% of this fund is invested in companies involved in issues of concern to you.*

What does this investment profile report mean? It basically shows how much of your current fund is invested in companies involved in issues of concern to you.

For example, Fidelity Magellan invests 24.48% of its assets in companies involved in the Same sex life style issue. This means that for every $100 you have invested in the fund, as much as $24.48 is invested in companies whose involvement with Same sex life style issue might be inconsistent with your personal values.

Under current investment screening technology, international/foreign funds can only be screened for three issues (alcohol, gambling, and tobacco). Bonds are not currently screened.

*Although MoneyAndValues.com exercises due care in compiling this data, MoneyAndValues.com makes no warranty, express or implied, as to the accuracy, completeness, or usefulness of this value rating percentage.

Information obtained from Values Investment Forum, June 1999.

Technology has been the primary catalyst for the development of values-based investing. Just log on to the Values

Financial Network Web site, <http://www.vfn.net/>. You will see an option, Investment Research. When you click on this button, you can type in the name of your mutual fund. In a few seconds you will see exactly what percentage of your investment is supporting companies involved in abortion, pornography, gambling, and the gay lifestyle, or which are involved in the manufacture or distribution of alcohol and tobacco products. The result may shock you. The question you must ask yourself is, "Does this investment reflect my values?" If so, great. My compliments. If not, you'll sleep better by investing with ones that do.

How Do You Screen a Mutual Fund?

If you have determined that values-based investing is important to you, then you should make a regular habit of monitoring your mutual funds. The ratings are dynamic. Your mutual fund may be in the positive category at one time and in the negative a few weeks later.

The Values Investment Forum (VIF) is quickly becoming the standard for values-based research services in the financial services industry. The Domini Group and a few others have been handling socially responsible research for more than two decades. As I pointed out earlier, however, this research is concerned with socially liberal issues. No group has specifically focused on the socially conservative investment marketplace and provided screening services for those investments. About two years ago, VIF developed their process. They have a prominent board of directors and a highly competent research staff. Together they are responsible for defining what issues will be screened and how they will execute the screening process.

Having a high quality research team is of paramount importance to the integrity of the whole concept of values-based investing. The two most critical aspects of the screening process are (1) objectivity and (2) consistency. If there is a failure at either of these junctions, the integrity of the entire process breaks down.

For example, let's take the issue of abortion. One mutual fund in particular caters to the Christian community but does not screen out companies that make large donations to Planned Parenthood. To me and to the Values Investment Forum, this type of screening is inconsistent and subjective. The definition of a company that fails the abortion screen for VIF would include whether this company either produces abortifacients (chemicals used to cause an abortion) or was a substantial financial contributor to Planned Parenthood during the last five years.

Definition of the Screening Issues and Their Parameters

Patrick Johnson, president of the Values Investment Forum (VIF) writes, "This is probably one of the most difficult tasks in the process: determining not only which broad issues to cover, but also defining the various parameters under each issue. VIF currently covers six screening issues: abortion, pornography, same-sex lifestyles (known as cultural screens) and alcohol, gaming, and tobacco (known as consumer screens). We then take each issue and define the specific parameters that will be covered. For example, the abortion issue contains six parameters ranging from manufacturers of abortifacients to corporate contributors to Planned Parenthood, the largest abortion provider in the country.

"We also seek the assistance of our nationally-known advisory board to determine which issues and parameters to cover and the depth of coverage. Our Director of Research has a master of theology as well as an extensive business background which aids in this process."

Conducting Primary Research
Around the Issues and Parameters

VIF, Johnson continues, believes that in order for the highest levels of integrity to be attained and maintained in the research process, one must rely principally upon primary sources and not secondary sources in the research process.

VIF has a staff of researchers who have become specialists on the issues and the companies that are involved with socially conservative issues. This staff uses a variety of sources of both primary and secondary information to identify companies that potentially fail our screens. This information is then entered into their expanding database of researched companies.

A company is not reported as failing a screen until this failure has been confirmed by a primary source (i.e., a source directly related to the company such as the company's 10K, annual report, Web site, or direct communication with the company via telephone or mail).

Continuous Updating of the Research

Changes occur in both the issues and the corporations that are covered by the research. According to Johnson, recent developments with respect to the abortifacient nature of contraceptives, for example, require continuous oversight and involvement with the issue of abortion. In addition, corporations are continuously merging, acquiring, and divesting themselves of companies, and all this requires continuous monitoring. VIF's research staff uses a variety of sources such as the *Wall Street Journal Interactive* and financial publications to stay abreast of developments within the corporate world. VIF also works closely with socially conservative organizations to stay informed of developments in each of the issues covered by its research.

The primary research involves direct communication between VIF and the company to determine its business activities, products, and markets. With this primary information, VIF can determine if this company is involved with any of the industries under scrutiny. The secondary research involves obtaining information from other sources such as Christian watchdog agencies like American Family Association, Provita Advisors, and Life Decisions International and from industry trade journals or other published information.

Once the list is compiled of companies traded on the New York Stock Exchange or NASDAQ and involved in any of the six issues, these companies are packaged into a software program that interfaces directly with another program that lists the holdings of each specific mutual fund. Whereas the first program is proprietary, the latter software interface is commercially available. As helpful as technology is, ultimately it is the research that is the key to maintaining the depth and overall quality of the screening process.

While the task to monitor these funds appears huge, it's actually quite manageable. There are about 2,600 companies on the New York Stock Exchange. Some of these companies are typically not going to have any involvement with the six issues of the screening process, such as oil drilling companies, for example. A large percentage of these companies can be segregated out of constant monitoring simply because of the nature of their business or product.

Some sectors of the industry, on the other hand, are ripe with the need for close and constant values research. For example, food and beverage are important when considering alcohol and tobacco. Within these industries there are such common violators—such as Seagram's or Anheuser-Busch—that they do not need to be checked each month.

On the other hand, a huge conglomerate like AT&T needs to be monitored every month. From time to time, AT&T has donated to Planned Parenthood.

When you combine the companies with no possible concern on the six issues and the companies that are consistent violators, the companies that remain fluctuate. As a result, the screening process becomes manageable.

Does Values-Based Investing Cause Investment Return to Suffer?

The answer is no—good news to investors who are concerned about values. According to Dr. Paul Farrell of CBS Marketwatch, "Whether you're conservative or liberal, you're likely to have some convictions about many things in life. And over 15 percent of us are now investing our money based on those principles."

In his article, Dr. Farrell gives an illustration, "For example, you may want to avoid investing in the Oakmark Fund (OAKMX), an otherwise great no-load favorite. Why? Well, if you check Oakmark's holdings, you will find about 10 percent of Oakmark's $6 billion is invested in Phillip Morris, whose sales were $84 billion in 1998, including half of all America's tobacco sales. Moreover, the company owned the Miller Brewery. The fact that at least $1 billion, or 15 percent of Oakmark's investments are in tobacco and alcohol apparently doesn't bother most of Oakmark's investors." On the other hand, I personally doubt that the majority of Oakmark's investors know about these holdings.

"The fact that over 70 percent of the most popular screened mutual funds finished 1998 as top performers should be the last nail in the coffin of the tired myth that responsible investing means sacrificing returns," according to Steve Schueth, president of the Social Investment Forum.

There is a mistaken notion that if you include your values in the investment decisions, then you will have to give up performance. That simply is not true. The Values Investment Forum and other research companies have proven that there is no correlation between including your values in the investment decision-making and poor performance. We think that to the extent that you include your values in the investment decisions, then you actually enhance the overall return of your portfolio, because at that point you begin to achieve not only a financial return but a moral return as well.

We talk about getting a double bottom line. The first bottom line is the investment performance. The second bottom line is the moral return. We don't think that investors should settle for anything less.

Why Haven't I Heard of Values-Based Investing?

The one word answer to why you haven't heard of values-based investing is *technology*. Until recently we have not had the technical capability to amass all the research necessary to screen 3,000 or 4,000 companies.

For example, there are 10,000 mutual funds. The screening will be done on about 4,000 companies. You have to take the 10,000 mutual funds and put them against the 4,000 companies that are screened. It's been a tremendous technological challenge. But in recent years, with the advent of the microcomputer, that technological challenge has been met. Keep in mind that mutual funds were not even invented until 1924. Additionally, it's been a recent phenomenon that people have had discretionary money to invest. For example, 401(k) and other cash-balance retirement plans are a fairly recent development in the employment world, and only in the last decade have they become popular.

We are not crusading in the sense that we are telling people what their values should be. That is something that should be developed within the family and within the religious and political arenas. Rather, an initiative like the Values Financial Network simply wants to act as a mirror, reflecting back to you exactly what you look like from a values-investing standpoint.

According to the Values Investment Forum, out of the top five most popular mutual funds in the United States, over $400 billion of those investments are channeled directly into industries such as abortion, pornography, gambling, alcohol, tobacco, and companies that promote a same-sex lifestyle. That $400 billion probably represents millions of investors who are unaware that their money is helping to support causes that they abhor.

Your options for finding out how to align your money with your values include both the do-it-yourself option utilizing the Internet site mentioned earlier, as well as the option of professional financial assistance. If your financial adviser is a member of the Values Financial Network, he will have all the tools and resources at his fingertips to assist you. He will be able to accomplish some in-depth screening—much more than you can do on the Internet site. On the other hand, if he is not a member of the Values Financial Network, there is a high probability that he will not have the tools necessary to find out whether your investments align with your values.

Ask your financial planner about his resources. If he is not a member of the VFN, encourage him to call 1-888-346-8258. Through the VFN, your adviser will be able to access what he needs to be able to help you align your money with your values.

As the executive director of VFN, my passion is making sure that financial advisers add one more question to their suitability checklist: "Do my client's investments match his personal values?" After all, investment return and living out your personal values should not be exclusive propositions.

It's Easy to Get Involved

If you are a do-it-yourself investor, as are about 20% of the investing public, you can log onto http://www/vfn.net/. You can contact your existing financial advisor, if you have one, or call Values Financial Network at 1-888-346-8258 and find out if there is a Values Financial Network-affiliated financial adviser in your area.

Keep in mind that if your financial professional is not a member of the Values Financial Network, he may not be familiar with the idea of values-based investing. Remember, the Values Financial Network is the financial services resource center for values-based financial advisers. VFN has the necessary resources to help you in the stewardship process of your financial resources by showing you how to align your money with your values so that in the end your money will produce both a *financial* return and a *moral* return.

Spread the Word in Your Churches

If you've been motivated with what you've learned about values-based investing, imagine the reaction from your pastor who might learn that his retirement program has 40 cents of every dollar invested in abortion, pornography, and gambling. Your church and pastor, along with other Christians, will be acutely interested in this concept. To help you in your attempt to educate others, VFN offers seminars, brochures, and information to churches, primarily through a network of financial advisers.

In the final analysis, to the extent that Christians align their financial planning and investing with their values, hundreds of billions of dollars will be taken out of those industries that are totally contrary to Christian values. We believe this course of responsible investing is something that has intuitive appeal for socially conservative Christians, just as it has for socially liberal investors for decades.

In the spring of 1999, we met with the chancellor of a Christian university about the idea of adding values-based investment options to the university's retirement plan. We began by educating the chancellor and his staff about the extent to which their current plan's investment options might be invested in companies that manufacture abortion drugs, publish or distribute pornography, advocate a same-sex corporate policy, or promote the gambling industry. To illustrate our point, we showed them the extent to which the Fidelity Magellan Fund (the largest mutual fund in the industry) is invested in these issues. A full 40% of the fund was invested in five of the six issues we screened for. At this, the chancellor turned to his CFO and asked, "Gerry, what fund family do we offer in our retirement plan?" The chancellor was to my left at the head of the large table in the boardroom, and the CFO was to my right at the other end. I watched as the CFO swallowed hard and said, "Fidelity." With that, the chancellor became animated, leaning forward toward his CFO, and said loudly, "Our employees would lynch me if they knew what they were investing in!"

This happens all the time. It's an education issue. You, like this chancellor, have two options. You can either follow Pontius Pilate's example and simply wash your hands and let things follow their natural tendencies (whether right or wrong), or you can be like Martin Luther who proclaimed to the world, "Here I stand. I can do no other." The bottom line is that your values are either the compass from which you direct your life, or they are nothing more than window dressing.

The sun was not up yet as Libby and I closed the front door and walked toward our car. We buckled our seat belts, and I turned the ignition and then backed out of the driveway. We were both very excited, but also equally anxious. We had done this before, almost a year earlier to the day. Libby was almost thirty-seven weeks into her pregnancy, and we had scheduled a C-section for this morning, Friday, August 6, 1999. The actual due date wasn't for another three weeks, but because we never found out why our son, Forrest, died in his last couple of weeks of gestation, the doctors suggested we move the delivery date up.

The drive to Baptist Hospital was uneventful and peaceful. We were both in deep thought and deep prayer. Would something go wrong again? What if it did? Could we handle the devastation of losing another baby right at the end of a normal pregnancy?

We checked into the hospital. Same hallways, same look, a lot of the same faces. I allowed myself a glance at the bed where the last sonogram was done a year earlier, where the doctor pronounced our son dead. Now I watched as nurses came and went from the surgery prep room, sticking, poking, and probing Libby in preparation for the surgery. Then in came Fred Schwarz, the nurse anesthetist who also happened to be a client of mine. He was there last year, too. Smiling and excited, he moved the IV toward Libby and asked, "Are you hungry? Here comes your breakfast." After skillfully performing his duties, he shut the door and asked if we wanted to join him in a word of prayer. I was so pleased Fred asked. I had wanted to do the same, but I knew I would choke up as the first words rolled off my lips. We held hands and Fred began. "Lord, we ask you to be with Stephen and Libby at this time of great emotion..."

Things moved rapidly after that, and I put on the surgical coverings and mask. I followed the nurses into the cold surgery room. Fred grabbed a chair and said, "Here, Stephen. Sit right here so you can hold Libby's hand and talk with her." Soon, Dr. Piper and Dr. Schlechter walked in and took control of the room. I looked around and had such a feeling of déjà vu. The exact room, the same anesthesiologist, the same doctors as one year ago. But what about the outcome? Would it be the same?

The doctors, and nurses began. It was not long before Dr. Piper joyously announced that we were close, and sure enough, momentarily thereafter, I watched as my daughter was born! The room erupted with cries of excitement and relief, and Ann-Rachel Darling Bolt announced her life with a cry, the most wonderful cry I will ever hear. I was beyond emotion. I was stunned.

The nurses allowed Libby only a few seconds to see her daughter before they raced her out to neonatal care. As Libby was wheeled to her recovery room, I walked out and down the hall, still in my surgical clothes. I looked up and saw Phyllis Keller, Libby's mother, and Ruby. Phyllis excitedly and anxiously asked, "Is everything all right? Is Libby OK? What about the baby?" I was so caught up with emotion that I had tears in my eyes and couldn't talk. This only made Libby's mother even more anxious. I finally was able to whisper, "Yes, Libby is fine." At this Phyllis said, "What about the baby? Is she all right?" All I could do was nod. At that, all three of us embraced tightly.

Libby and I were able to spend some quality time in her hospital room enjoying each other and this new life that God had blessed us with. One evening, as Libby lay resting and Ann-Rachel was nestled warmly in my arms, I relaxed into the peace and comfort of the moment. I settled back into a soft chair. I looked down at the face of this beautiful child. My mind wandered, and I began thinking about this tiny baby, only two days old, growing into a toddler, a child, a young adult, and then having her own family. I thought about what I could do as a trusted parent to help her in that life. What important principles would I teach her?

More than anything else, I will teach her about values. Life is nothing if it is not about values. Choices, noise, competing ideas, temptations, frustration, pressure, stress. These are part of life too, unavoidable consequences of living in a fallen world, the world Adam and Eve chose when their pride got the best of them and they disobeyed their Creator. But Ann-Rachel will also learn about God's love, so immense that He sought peace with His creation, even after His creation chose sin. Thousands of years later and after many rebellious acts, God still went after us. I will teach her about the final act of God's redemption, the sacrifice of His pure, sinless Son to a horrible death by crucifixion to once and for all pay the price of sin for all mankind. And I will teach her then about the resurrection, how Jesus became the firstborn of the new life. She will learn about the Holy Spirit and the incredible power for living He provides. Most of all, Ann-Rachel will know that regardless of the failings of her parents and her friends, and regardless of the troubles, heartache, and sin she will face in her life, God will never, ever leave her. He will always be with her, always perfect, always in love with her.

It is from the vastness of supernatural love that Ann-Rachel will learn how to live a life of purpose, so that she, through the indwelling of the Holy Spirit, can reflect the image of this wonderful God in all her life. The power of the almighty God that created the universe is the same power that nurtures us in life and gives us the power to live life on purpose, even in a sinful world.

Will Ann-Rachel choose to be a doctor, a teacher, a homemaker? What will her interests and avocations be? How much money will she need, and when will she need it? The answers to these questions are for her to make, and she has the freedom and power to develop her life however she pleases.

These issues will be the foundation from which she will develop her life. And the result of her soul-searching will create the need for her to manage her financial resources in a way that provides sufficient money. I hope to serve Ann-Rachel as her consultant, helping her to weave her own life of purpose and meaning, taking into account first her talents, adding to those her interests, and then finally helping her consider her opportunities. I will also counsel her to develop a specific financial plan to support that life, and I'll show her how to manage it in tandem with her changing life goals, so that her life goals and her financial plan are always synchronized.

Finally, I will counsel her to think about how reflecting her values goes well beyond her own life. How her money is invested will ultimately fund *somebody's* values, so I'll teach her to invest her money to reflect *her* values. Money is the economic oxygen of business, and if she is not careful, she will unwittingly provide oxygen to abortion, pornography, gambling, and the institutionalization of a same-sex lifestyle by funding companies who promote those values.

As Patrick Johnson, president of Values Investment Forum, syllogistically puts it, "Everything that exists is owned by God. He has breathed life into us and given each of us charge of various resources. Before we invest we must ask ourselves, "Would God want to own this company? After all, it is His money we are investing."

Patrick's illustration offers a much clearer guide to aligning values with investing than what we are most often confronted with. Few Christians would argue that buying stock outright in a company that publishes pornography sold in adult bookstores is an appropriate purchase "on behalf of God." But how many Christians who buy shares in mutual funds, IRAs, and 401(k) plans even bother to check to see which companies' stocks are in those mutual funds? Just because those stocks are purchased as a "package" in a mutual fund instead of individually, does not make our stewardship responsibility any less important.

What would I like for my tiny seven-pound, two-and-one-half-ounce little girl to ultimately do or be in her life? What about her life choices would satisfy me, her caring father? That answer is actually quite simple. My satisfaction will overflow regardless of what she chooses in her life, so long as those choices reflect purpose. And choosing to live a life on purpose begins with a life in Christ and follows with choices based on stewardship, managing resources, opportunities, and time in ways that reflect the character of our awesome God. And that life is the *ultimate life.*

I have similar aspirations to teach everyone who reads this book. As you have read through the pages of this book, I hope it has triggered you to revisit your key purpose in life, starting with the right foundation—a life in

Christ. From there, living each day on purpose, making a truly fulfilling life from all of the resources that God has entrusted to you. If you have not yet taken the personal inventory that I outlined at the end of chapter 1, now is an excellent time to turn to those pages and begin to apply this information to your individual circumstances and life.

If you don't make the conscious decision to be proactive, then you will have effectively made the choice simply to exist. Remember, the right order is life, purpose, plan, money. And that order does not require any money to get started.

If you choose to follow the advice in these pages, you will find a more abundant life through an intimate connection to God. As Jesus promised in Matthew 13:11-12, "The knowledge of the secrets of the kingdom of heaven has been given to you, but not to them. Whoever has will be given more, and he will have an abundance. Whoever does not have, even what he has will be taken from him."

The abundant life can be yours—if you use what you've been given. From that spiritual foundation, begin by determining your financial goals, then move joyfully and purposefully ahead to live out your life in the most fulfilling way.

As you do, you will discover that you, too, have learned how to have *Money for Life*.

Personal
Information Form

Objectives and Resources

I. RETIREMENT PLANNING

If you retired today, what monthly income would you want?

$ _____

Age when you desire to retire _____

Age when your spouse desires to retire _____

II. COLLEGE FUNDING

Amount you expect to contribute per child per year for

college $ _____

Income Information

Client Earned Income—Self-Employed   Yes_____ No____

$ _____

Spouse Earned Income—Self-Employed   Yes_____ No____

$ _____

Client Social Security Income $ _____

Spouse Social Security Income $ _____

Interest/Dividends $ _____

Rental Property Gain (Loss) $ _____

Other Income $ _____

Deductions $ _____

Exemptions $ _____

Filing Status   ___Single   ___Married - Joint

           ___Married - Separate   ___Head of Household

Current Year Projected Income _____

  Client $_____

  Spouse $ _____

Life Insurance

1. Company _____

  *Type _____

  Insured/Owner _____

  Beneficiary_____

  Face Amount $ _____

  Annual Premium $ _____

  Loans $ _____

  Current Cash Value $ _____

2. Company _____

  *Type _____

  Insured/Owner _____

  Beneficiary_____

  Face Amount $ _____

  Annual Premium $ _____

  Loans $ _____

  Current Cash Value $ _____

3. Company _____

   *Type _____

   Insured/Owner _____

   Beneficiary_____

   Face Amount $ _____

   Annual Premium $ _____

   Loans $ _____

   Current Cash Value $ _____

4. Company _____

   *Type _____

   Insured/Owner _____

   Beneficiary_____

   Face Amount $ _____

   Annual Premium $ _____

   Loans $ _____

   Current Cash Value $ _____

     *W=Whole Life   F=Fixed   V=Variable Universal Life   T=Term

Disability Insurance

Company _____

Insured _____

Annual Premium $_____

Monthly Benefit $ _____

Waiting Period _____

Benefit Duration _____

Other Insurance

Health

Company _____

Annual premium _____

Insured _____

Coverage Type _____

Coinsurance % _____

Max Out-of-Pocket $_____

Lifetime Limit $_____

Deduct./Person $ _____

Deduct./Family $ _____

Personal Liability

Company _____

Annual Premium $_____

Max Coverage $_____

Deductible $_____

Medical Supplement

Company _____

Annual Premium $_____

Nursing Home/Long-Term Care

Company _____

Annual Premium $_____

Investment Assets

Asset Name _____

*Type _____

Owner _____

Current Value $ _____

Monthly Addition $ _____

Rate of Return _____

Maturity Date _____

Notes _____

Asset Name _____

*Type _____

Owner _____

Current Value $ _____

Monthly Addition $ _____

Rate of Return _____

Maturity Date _____

Notes _____

Asset Name _____

*Type _____

Owner _____

Current Value $ _____

Monthly Addition $ _____

Rate of Return _____

Maturity Date _____

Notes _____

Asset Name _____

*Type _____

Owner _____

Current Value $ _____

Monthly Addition $ _____

Rate of Return _____

Maturity Date_____

Notes _____

Asset Name_____

*Type _____

Owner _____

Current Value $ _____

Monthly Addition $ _____

Rate of Return _____

Maturity Date_____

Notes _____

Asset Name_____

*Type _____

Owner _____

Current Value $ _____

Monthly Addition $ _____

Rate of Return _____

Maturity Date_____

Notes _____

* 1=Savings/Checking, 2=Certificate of Deposit, 3=Fixed Annuity,
  5=Bonds, 6=Notes Receivable, 7=Energy (Oil, Gas), 8=Stocks,
  9=Mutual Funds, 10=Land,11=Rental Real Estate, 12=Agriculture,
  13=Gold/Silver/Gems/Coins, 14=Business, 15=Other

Retirement Assets

Asset Name _____

*Type _____

Owner _____

Account Balance $ _____

Ongoing Cont. or % of Pay _____

Rate of Return _____

Notes _____

Asset Name _____

*Type _____

Owner _____

Account Balance $ _____

Ongoing Cont. or % of Pay _____

Rate of Return _____

Notes _____

Asset Name _____

*Type _____

Owner _____

Account Balance $ _____

Ongoing Cont. or % of Pay _____

Rate of Return _____

Notes _____

* I=IRA, E=SEP, K=KEOGH, F=401(K), P=Pension/Profit Sharing, D=Deferred Comp, S=Salary Savings, O=Other, R=Roth, M=Simple

Client: Do you receive company match?   Yes____   No____

Spouse: Do you receive company match?   Yes____   No____

Miscellaneous and Personal Assets

Residence_____

Owner _____

Market Value $ _____

Notes _____

Personal Property _____

Owner _____

Market Value $ _____

Notes _____

RVs/Boats _____

Owner _____

Market Value $ _____

Notes _____

Autos _____

Owner _____

Market Value $ _____

Notes _____

Other _____

Owner _____

Market Value $ _____

Notes _____

Other _____

Owner _____

Market Value $ _____

Notes _____

Debts

Owner (Home Loan) _____

Current Balance $ _____

Monthly Payment $ _____

Original Amount Financed $ _____

Interest Rate _____

Date Opened _____

Original Term _____

Owner (Home Equity Loan) _____

Current Balance $ _____

Monthly Payment $ _____

Original Amount Financed $ _____

Interest Rate _____

Date Opened _____

Original Term _____

Owner (Investment Loan) _____

Current Balance $ _____

Monthly Payment $ _____

Original Amount Financed $ _____

Interest Rate _____

Date Opened _____

Original Term _____

Owner (Charge Cards) _____

Current Balance $ _____

Monthly Payment $ _____

Original Amount Financed $ _____

Interest Rate _____

Date Opened _____

Original Term _____

Owner (Personal Loan) _____

Current Balance $ _____

Monthly Payment $ _____

Original Amount Financed $ _____

Interest Rate _____

Date Opened _____

Original Term _____

Owner (Auto Loan) _____

Current Balance $ _____

Monthly Payment $ _____

Original Amount Financed $ _____

Interest Rate _____

Date Opened _____

Original Term _____

Owner (Other) _____

Current Balance $ _____

Monthly Payment $ _____

Original Amount Financed $ _____

Interest Rate _____

Date Opened _____

Original Term _____

Does your monthly home loan payment include escrow for taxes
and insurance? Yes_____ No____

Amount of real estate taxes per year $_____

Living Expenses Worksheet

Auto—Gas	$ _____
Auto—Maintenance	$ _____
Auto—Insurance	$ _____
Homeowners Insurance	$ _____
House—Maintenance	$ _____
Rent	$ _____
Utilities	$ _____
Food	$ _____
Clothing	$ _____
Entertainment	$ _____
Allowances	$ _____
Child Support	$ _____
Childcare	$ _____
Education	$ _____
Fees/Dues/Memberships	$ _____
Gifts	$ _____
Vacations	$ _____
Contribution/Tithe	$ _____
Personal Care	$ _____
Accounting/Legal Fees	$ _____
Out-of-Pocket Medical Costs	$ _____
Pets	$ _____
Other_____	$ _____
Other_____	$ _____
Other_____	$ _____
Total	$ _____

Risk Profile
Questionnaire

Name: _____

Home Address: _____

_____

_____

Home Phone: _____ Home Fax: _____

Date of Birth: _____ S.S./Tax ID: _____

Occupation: _____

Employer: _____

Work Address: _____

_____

_____

Work Phone: _____ Work Fax: _____

Spouse's Name: _____

Date of Birth: _____ S.S./Tax ID: _____

Occupation: _____ Employer: _____

Children or Dependents:

Name _____   Birth Date _____

Name _____   Birth Date _____

Name _____   Birth Date _____

Annual Income: $ _____

Estimated Net Worth: $_____

Estimated Tax Bracket: _____

I. Client Profile — What Type of Investor Are You?

Determining your personal risk tolerance and expected rates of return are essential in establishing your investment objectives. Therefore, we need your input, which will provide us with the foundation for (a) determining your investment objectives, (b) identifying your risk tolerance, and (c) understanding your performance expectations. Effective communication is vital in effective investment management. The more we know about you, your current financial situation, and goals, the better strategies we can identify. Your investment portfolio will be customized and tailored to your personal goals and objectives and specifically allocated based on the facts and preferences you provide in the pages that follow.

1. What is the approximate amount of assets to be initially invested? $ _____

2. How are these assets currently being managed? _____

_____

_____

_____

3. Please indicate the intended use of your investment portfolio.

__Wealth-Building   ____ Future Capital Expenditures

__Current Income   (Residence, etc.)

__Dependents' Education   ____ Purchasing Power

__Satisfy Investment Policy   (Maintenance)

__Retirement   ____ Other _____

_____

_____

4. What percentage of your total investable assets will be
   represented by this portfolio? (This is vital information in
   compiling your asset allocation analysis.)

   __ _75% to 100%   _____25% to 50%

   ____50% to 75%   _____Less than 25%

   If known, please indicate the exact percentage: _____

5. Please describe the general composition of your current
   overall portfolio (including principal residence):

   Bank Accounts $_____

   CDs $_____

   Money Market Funds $_____

   Stocks $_____

   Bonds $_____

   Mutual Funds $_____

   Tax-Deferred Annuities $_____

   Life Insurance (Cash Value) $_____

   Investment Real Estate $_____

   Other (Please Specify) $_____

6. From your answer on #5, please indicate the split among the following types of accounts:

* Personal Nonretirement

Accounts $ _____

* Retirement Accounts

IRA/IRA Rollover $ _____

KEOGH $ _____

SEP $ _____

401(k)/403(b) $ _____

Other $ _____

7. Are there any constraints on your portfolio with regard to legal or tax consequences?   No_____ Yes_____

If yes, please explain: _____

_____

_____

8. Please estimate the contributions and/or withdrawals, if any, you anticipate making to your portfolio:

Year	Contributions	Withdrawals
1	$ _____	$_____
2	$ _____	$_____
3	$ _____	$_____
4	$ _____	$_____
5	$ _____	$_____

II. Investment Policy Nonfinancial Criteria

Investments are the economic oxygen of business. The dollars you invest will support businesses in various industries, many of which may not be consistent with your personal values (such as abortion, pornography, gambling, tobacco).

Would you like your personal values reflected in your investments? _____

If so, please indicate in general terms if those values are socially conservative or liberal. _____

Below is a list of values issues. Please indicate which issues are important to you in the composition of your investments.

Socially Conservative

Include	Exclude	N/A	
_____	_____	_____	Alcohol/Production and Distribution
_____	_____	_____	Fetal Research/Genetic Engineering
_____	_____	_____	Gambling
_____	_____	_____	Abortion
_____	_____	_____	Pornography
_____	_____	_____	Tobacco
_____	_____	_____	Same-Sex Lifestyle

Socially Liberal

_____	_____	_____	Military Contractors
_____	_____	_____	Environmentally Proactive
_____	_____	_____	Animal Testing/Research

_____	_____	_____

Management: Minority
Pro-active

_____	_____	_____

Nuclear Energy

_____	_____	_____

Fossil Fuel Production

_____	_____	_____

Alternative Energy

III. Investment Objective, Risk, Time, and Return Expectations

A. Investment Objective

Your investment objective summarizes the primary purpose of your investment portfolio. It serves to define how your assets should be managed. While asking yourself, "What do I want to accomplish with my investments?" check the on objective which best fits your purpose for investing.

_____ Preserve Asset Value

_____ Generate High Current Income

_____ Achieve Asset Growth with Moderate Current Income

_____ Achieve Strong Asset Growth with Nominal Income

_____ Achieve Maximum Asset Appreciation

B. Risk Tolerance

Investing in different asset classes and asset allocations can result in varying and occasionally wide fluctuations in the value of your portfolio over time. As a general rule, the more risk you are willing to accept, or the more volatility you can withstand, the higher the prospective rate of return you should be compensated with over a sufficiently long time horizon. Use the following ranges of volatility over a one-year time horizon to help determine a benchmark for the amount of risk you can tolerate, while keeping in mind the investment objective you determined in Section A.

Upside/Downside Potential	Potential Variance	Risk Tolerance
_____ 5%	0-5%	Very Low
_____ 10%	5-10%	Low
_____ 15%	10-15%	Moderate
_____ 20%	15-20%	Moderate-High
_____ Over 20%	Over 20%	High

C. TIME HORIZON

Your age and investment time horizon are important variables to consider when constructing you portfolio. Your portfolio should be considered within the context of a longer-term investment horizon. For example, for younger investors, a longer time frame enables them to benefit from strategies that may take many market cycles to be successful while undertaking greater risk. Conversely, investors near on in retirement may want to be more conservative in their investment selections to benefit from low investment risk. A specific time frame is also useful as a benchmark by which investment result can be assessed. With this in mind, place a mark next to the time frame that best corresponds to your profile.

_____ 0 - 1 Years

_____ 1 - 2 Years

_____ 2 - 4 Years

_____ 4 - 6 Years

_____ Over 6 Years

D. RETURN EXPECTATIONS

Construction of a strategic asset allocation is based upon your profile in regard to objective, risk tolerance, and time horizon, but is primarily driven by your expectations of performance. For example, it is not likely to construct an efficient portfolio with an objective of high current income, low risk tolerance and a two-year time horizon, where your return exception is greater than 15%. Likewise, you are shortchanging your portfolio if you have an objective of maximizing asset growth, a high tolerance for risk and a ten-year time horizon, while only expecting an annual rate return of 5%. To set a benchmark, select from the following range of returns the range that best describes your target rate of return on your portfolio, without considering inflation and taxes, in light of your responses to the other profile questions.

_____	5% to 7%
_____	7% to 9%
_____	9% to 11%
_____	11% to 13%
_____	Other : _____%